DAWN OF AMERICAN DEER HUNTING

VOLUME TWO
A PHOTOGRAPHIC ODYSSEY OF WHITETAIL HUNTING

To Richard Lindemann,
Here's to the greatest game
animal on Earth!   Best Wishes
                    Duncan Dobie

Copyright ©2018, Sporting Classics.

All rights reserved. No part of this book may be reproduced, stored or introduced into a retrieval system, or transmitted in any form by any means without written permission of the publisher.

Published by

117 Alpine Circle, Suite 500
Columbia, South Carolina 29223
(800) 849-1004 • www.SportingClassics.com

To order books or other products, call toll-free 1-800-849-1004
or visit us online at www.SportingClassicsStore.com.

All photos and graphics, unless noted, are credited to
Duncan Dobie's personal collection.

Library of Congress Control Number: 2016427599
ISBN-13: 978-0-9980309-0-6
ISBN-10: 0-9980309-0-2

Edited By Chuck Wechsler
Designed by Ryan Coleman

*For Katherine who, despite her grueling chemotherapy at age 13,
loved to sit in a deer stand with me in the fall woods.*

ABOUT THE AUTHOR

Duncan Dobie has been a full-time outdoor writer since 1980. The author of more than 2,500 articles, his stories and photographs have appeared in numerous books, magazines and newspapers across the country. Most of his articles are about whitetails and whitetail hunting. Over the years, he has earned a reputation as being one of the nation's top authorities on the white-tailed deer.

Duncan has written 11 previous books, contributed to numerous others, and helped edit and produce a number of books for other writers. He served as editor of *North American Whitetail* magazine from 2004 until 2009. He lives in Marietta, Georgia, with his wife, Kappi. Writing this book has been a labor of love.

CONTENTS

FOREWORD……………………………………………………………………………7

INTRODUCTION……………………………………………………………………9

CHAPTER 1
   A TRIP BACK TO YESTERYEAR (PRE-1900)……………………………13

CHAPTER 2
   THE GILDED AGE OF WHITETAIL HUNTING (EARLY 1900S)……………29

CHAPTER 3
   DREAMS, DUST AND HARD WORK: THE MAGIC OF DEER CAMP……………43

CHAPTER 4
   MOON OF THE RUTTING STAG……………………………………………55

CHAPTER 5
   DEER TRACKS MAKE MIGHTY THIN SOUP………………………………69

THE ARTFUL WHITETAIL
   SPECIAL FULL-COLOR SECTION…………………………………………81

CHAPTER 6
   MR. BROWNING MADE A GUN
   JOHN MOSES BROWNING (1855-1926)……………………………………97

CHAPTER 7
   THE BUCK STOPS HERE:
   VERMONT'S AMAZING WHITETAIL HERITAGE……………………………113

CHAPTER 8
   WELCOME TO THE DEER WOODS:
   NOTHING LIKE IT IN THE WORLD…………………………………………123

A ROCKING-CHAIR RACK
  No matter how many opening days a seasoned hunter has experienced, no matter how many bucks he has under his belt, the feeling a true hunter gets deep in his being when he finally meets up with that one-in-a-million buck with a "rocking chair" rack is impossible to express in words. Holding his Savage Model 99EG II carbine close to his heart, this proud hunter stands in awe of his trophy. The bullet-riddled sign on the tree reads: "Camp Site." Photo circa late 1940s.

CHAPTER 9
A METHOD TO THE MADNESS:
DOGS, DEER DRIVES AND THE LUCK OF THE IRISH 135

CHAPTER 10
MADE IN THE U.S.A. – AMERICA'S NO. 1 BIG GAME SENSATION 145

CHAPTER 11
THE GIRLS OF AUTUMN:
FROM PETTICOATS TO SMOKING RIFLES 155

CHAPTER 12
MIXED BAG:
LURE OF THE WILDERNESS (OTHER SPECIES) 165

CHAPTER 13
A THOUSAND CAMPFIRES AGO 183

CHAPTER 14
BRAGGING RIGHTS 195

CHAPTER 15
LEGENDS OF THE HUNT:
MEN AND WOMEN WHO MADE THEIR MARK 207

CHAPTER 16
REFLECTIONS: SUNSETS AND NEW HORIZONS 235

FOREWORD
By Larry Weishuhn

KEEPING THE TRADITION ALIVE

Larry Weishuhn and the author glass for deer from a high knoll while hunting together on the Milk River in Montana.

To paraphrase the lyrics from a Waylon Jennings song, "Deer camps in Texas were my natural second home!"

Growing up in rural Texas, my family spent the first two weeks of the annual whitetail season at our "camphouse" hunting deer. We returned there during the Thanksgiving and Christmas holidays. Beyond hunting, some of my fondest early memories are of sitting around the fire listening to the hunting tales and seeing photos of deer taken by family, friends and ancestors.

Hardly a day has since passed I have not thought of hunting.

We hunters have a proud tradition and culture of being true conservationists, wisely managing wildlife and habitat for the perpetuation of both long into the future. We should always remember where we came from.

That is one of the many reasons why Duncan Dobie's passion for collecting and sharing photos of past hunters is paramount to all who love the chase and the camaraderie associated with the hunting culture.

I grew up reading folklore stories by J. Frank Dobie, a college professor and South Texas rancher. Years ago, when I read a deer hunting article by Duncan Dobie, I wondered if there might be a family connection. There is! Duncan Dobie's family roots are proudly in Texas.

From the first of his articles and ensuing books, I loved Duncan's writing style and the topics he chose to write about. He was genuine! When I finally had the opportunity to sit and visit with Duncan, I gained even greater respect for him and his writings. Beyond whitetail hunting, we talked about a shared interest in vintage hunting photos.

After visiting on and off for several years, we finally shared a hunting camp during the First Annual Versus Whitetail Challenge. This friendly competition brought together four noted hunters on the historic Yturria Ranch in the Brush Country of South Texas. Versus was then the premier outdoor television network.

The early season hunt was tough; summertime temperatures and extremely thick thornbrush. Duncan hunted hard, but wisely. He waited until the last hour of the hunt to take a buck, which may well be the oldest whitetail I have ever seen as a hunter and wildlife biologist. Quite frankly, knowing his love of whitetails and passion for hunting mature bucks, I expected no less of him. To me, Duncan should have been the obvious winner.

In 2015, when I heard Duncan had released *Dawn of American Deer Hunting,* I was thrilled. I could not wait to see the photos he had accumulated and included. I was not disappointed! My copy is getting a bit ragged due to the many times I have read his narratives and studied and admired the vintage photos.

Thankfully, Duncan has completed, this book, his anxiously awaited compilation of vintage deer hunting photos complimented by his enjoyable, highly readable narratives. His first photographic whitetail hunting history book was fabulous. Whatever the next level of superlative is, this pictorial history epic is it. Sit back, enjoy, dream and recall!

Larry Weishuhn (right) and Duncan Dobie on a trophy whitetail hunt in northeastern Montana.

INTRODUCTION
By Duncan Dobie

PHOTOGRAPHIC TREASURES

Nothing elevates a writer's self esteem regarding his work more than receiving letters or phone calls praising certain stories or columns he's penned. When the first edition of *Dawn of American Deer Hunting* came out, I was quite amazed by the response. Nothing I had ever written received the kind of positive reception and praise from hunters across the country. *Dawn* was my 10th book, and nothing close to this had ever happened before.

The book came out in December 2015, and by a stroke of luck, I happened to have a story in the January 2016 issue of *American Hunter*. That story featured about a dozen photos and captions from the book. The magazine went out to subscribers a few days before Christmas in 2015, and I immediately started receiving book orders by the dozen from hunters and NRA members across the country. I was flattered and astonished. This continued for the first four or five months of 2016.

After receiving the book, many of the readers who initially placed orders bought one or more additional copies for friends and relatives. I also received numerous letters asking when I was going to come out with a new edition. Well here it is.

I have always loved old hunting stories and photos—the classic guns, the times, the romance of early hunting camps and scenarios, anything having to do with deer hunting. Looking at an old photo is like finding a beautiful arrowhead. You pick up an arrowhead, study it for a moment, and wonder how another human being could have so perfectly fashioned such a functional work of art. You come to the realization that a person who lived on this earth—a hunter from long ago not unlike yourself—once fashioned this arrowhead from a piece of rock.

That arrowhead becomes a living, breathing symbol in your hand. Your imagination begins to take over, and you wonder... how did it end up in this place? Did that hunter of long ago lose it in his travels or did he miss a deer with it? How old was he? Did he have a family, a wife? What tribe was he from? Was he a good hunter? A million unanswered questions flash through your mind.

That treasured piece of rock will be taken home and put in a special place because it's worth more than gold. Every time you pick it up, hold it and admire it, the spirit of the hunter who once owned it surges through you because the flame can never be fully extinguished.

The same is true with old hunting photos. You flip through an aged scrapbook and come to a weathered black-and-white photo of a proud young man posed with his deer. You immediately begin to realize this image represents a living, breathing human being who once lived on this earth and had many of the same aspirations as you do now. For a moment in time, you put yourself in his place and wonder about the times he lived in, the kind of rifle he was using, what the deer was doing when he shot it. Was this his first buck?

In a way, history is repeating itself because now—100 years later—you find yourself doing the same things this young man did. Just like the arrowhead, that photo becomes a treasure from the past and a living shrine to the indomitable American spirit of long ago.

I hope that all the photographs in this book will be treasures from the past for those who look at them and study them. I hope you will cherish some of the stories behind the photos just like I do. These old photos are such a rich part of our deer hunting heritage.

As in the first book, writing the captions for these photos was a labor of love. I spent many hours researching old guns and facts, and I made every attempt to be as accurate as possible. In the first book, I made a few mistakes, and believe me, I heard about them from readers. I'm sure the same thing will happen here because many readers of this book have far more knowledge about firearms than I do.

You will find three photos in this book that appeared in the first book. Two of them ran without captions—the cover photo and the photo on page 8 of the first book. The captions are so important I wanted readers to see them, so I included those photos again. The third photo, in Chapter 11, depicts a young girl from Maine standing beside a large buck she shot with her father's lever-action rifle. I identified the rife as a Winchester, when in fact it is clearly a Marlin. Boy, did I hear about that. J. Scott Olmsted, editor of *American Hunter* magazine (where the photo appeared with my story), even corrected my mistake in a later issue after a reader had written in.

I hope you enjoy the photos in this book as much as I enjoyed putting them together and trying to retell some of the stories they tell. Some of them are really amazing.

Every photo and every hunter in that photo has a story to tell. It really is a gift to be able to go back in time and relive part of that story through old photographs. One hundred years from now, will people be looking at old photos of you and me and doing the same thing? I truly hope so, because it is so important to document our rich hunting history.

Whitetail hunters are the luckiest people on earth. I wish everyone could experience a small taste of deer camp, a small taste of the incredible tradition we share each fall. If they could, I believe it might easily change the world for the better.

Lastly, I want to thank Chuck Wechsler, Ryan Coleman and Duncan Grant at *Sporting Classics* magazine for believing in this project and allowing my dream for this book to become a reality. Thank you from the bottom of my heart.

God bless America's white-tailed deer and God bless the U.S.A.!

THE DEER HUNTER
Famous magazine illustrator Lynn Bogue Hunt created this gouache drawing for a book published in 1904.

"If any one animal is more responsible for the success of America's early colonization, it is the deer, which provided sustenance for the spread of civilization along the East Coast and for its march over the Appalachians and across the river, to the vast and unspoiled hinterlands beyond. This nation built its first sinew and bone on venison and made its first clothes of buckskin."

Charles Elliott
Gone Huntin' (1954)

"THE HUNTERS, THE BROTHERS."
In addition to the day's bounty, Dad is carrying an old double-barreled shotgun with rabbit ears that no doubt has fetched its share of venison over the years. The boy appears to be holding a single-shot shotgun. It could well be a Remington Model 1893 20-gauge (the cocking lever on the left side is not visible). What a day for a young lad to share with his father! Stereoview by B.W. Kilburn, circa 1888.

CHAPTER 1

A TRIP BACK TO YESTERYEAR (PRE-1900)

Why are American deer hunters so infatuated with the past? What is it about looking at old pictures from yesteryear that stirs our very being? Hunting touches the soul. When we go back in time and see how our grandfathers and great grandfathers took to the woods and chased after the same elusive animal we chase today, in the same woods they hunted 100 years ago, the spiritual connection is all powerful. It nourishes and feeds the modern soul. It really is who we are.

John Wootters is quoted in Chapter 14 as saying, "In the breast of almost every meat hunter there beats the heart of a secret, frustrated trophy hunter . . ."

Of course, the trophy is always in the eye of the beholder, but in truth, our passion for deer and deer hunting goes way beyond that. It goes beyond our American Indian forefathers who were the most spiritual hunters on Earth. It goes back to the dawn of time.

Although much of our connection with nature has been lost in the modern world, whitetails truly help us anchor our ties to the past so that we have a better understanding of who we are today, where we came from and what we aspire to be in the future. The past is important for many reasons, yet at times it is so easy to forget.

Because our deer hunting heritage has become ingrained in our American psyche for many generations, it's sometimes hard to believe that the first European-Americans who came to the New World didn't have a clue about how to hunt these clever animals. The immigrants had to be taught how to live off the land, and during that learning curve, a considerable number of them perished. But once they learned how to shoot a gun and develop the same woods skills and stealth used by their Indian teachers to track down a crafty and elusive prey, the love affair began, and venison became a staple across the Northeast. That love affair has continued right up to the present time.

It wasn't long before a unique breed of American pioneer was making his living hunting these New World deer for their delicious and nourishing flesh. Settlers, constantly pushing westward, also hunted this amazing animal because it provided a staple food supply and long-wearing buckskin duds. Later on, when hard money was scarce, its valuable skin provided a means of income to thousands of courageous traders up and down the Eastern Seaboard.

Today we may hunt for a different reason, but every time we set foot in the snow-filled woods and pick up the track of a woods-wise old buck, it's hard to follow that track without thinking about the incredible heritage our forefathers bequeathed us to cherish. These days, we are extremely fortunate to be able to take a glimpse back to the good old days through the many incredible photographs that were taken in the late 1800s and early 1900s and preserved. Hopefully, by occasionally taking a trip back to yesteryear, we will always recognize these treasures as the true gift they are.

ANTLER HAVEN
With a nice whitetail rack adorning the roof of one of the ramshackle sheds, these hunters don't seem to mind the rather primitive accommodations at their camp. It appears as though they are preparing to head for the woods with shotguns in hand. This scene could well be somewhere in the Adirondacks and these citified hunters are likely paying customers. As long as the food simmering on the fire is good and the hunting is productive, and as long as their pallets are warm and dry, the less-than-luxurious living conditions may be the least of their worries. Photo circa 1895.

A MIXED BAG

These hunters must have a golden horseshoe. Not only have they collected some outstanding bucks, but they've managed to bring down a bull moose and a wolf. The young sharpshooter sitting next to the dogs is holding a .22 rifle he's used to pick off some ruffed grouse and one or two snowshoe hares. Several lever-action Winchesters can be seen in the mix. This photo was probably taken in northern Minnesota or Wisconsin, circa 1895.

NIGHT HUNT BY BOAT

"Water-Hunting For Deer—A Night Scene On The River—Susquehanna, Pennsylvania," is an engraving that appeared in *The Illustrated London News* on April 11, 1857. It demonstrated how an American hunter sitting in the bow of a canoe with a fire torch behind him could sneak up on unsuspecting deer at night feeding along the water's edge. The fire torch gave off just enough light to faintly illuminate the deer. Illustration circa 1857.

TALLY HO
With a couple of Winchester '73s and several other Winchester lever guns for good company, these men are serious about collecting a passel of deer meat as they prepare to let the hounds loose and have a run through the swamp. They'll likely paddle their wooden bateaus to strategic spots where they can cut off deer trying to move

toward some dry hammocks. By nightfall, those boats may well be carrying a fair supply of venison. The thick stand of cypress trees indicates this photo was certainly taken in the Deep South, possibly in the bayous of Louisiana. Photo circa 1890.

"OUR CHRISTMAS HUNT, THE SNOW STORM."
A Man with a Winchester rifle takes a break from dragging his large-bodied deer through the snow. Stereoview by B.W. Kilburn, Littleton, NH, 1890

A.B. FROST ENGRAVING
Appearing in *Harper's Weekly* magazine on October 6, 1883, "Watering Deer—Indian Putting the Dogs On A Trail," depicts a hunter and his dogs preparing to follow freshly discovered deer tracks near a watering hole. Illustration circa 1883.

CAMP SERENITY U.S.A.

At first glance, this photo is reminiscent of a Union Army camp during the Civil War. Old Glory flies proudly over the large tent, and several of the men pictured might well be veterans of that late conflict. Discipline seems to rule in this tidy camp. We don't know the true name of this camp, but judging by its peaceful look, we might dub it Camp Serenity. While the meat pole sags with a hefty array of bucks, the old-timer (the "General") gathers the hounds together as the musket-wielding troops prepare for another afternoon skirmish with their four-legged quarry. Any bets on who might win the contest? Photo circa late 1800s.

THE ALL-AMERICAN WHITETAIL HUNTER

Whitetail hunters of yesteryear came from every strata of the economic scale. They were farmers and frontiersman who lived on the edge of civilization, and well-to-do doctors, lawyers and businessmen from the big city. These three "sports," proudly posing in a photo studio with their wilderness bounty probably came from a large city and traveled to the hinterlands by rail in the late 1880s. They could well afford to stay in a fine lodge and pay a guide for his services.

The quick-shooting 1873 Winchester repeater held by two of these men may have been the gun that "won the west," but it also played an important role in providing meat for hunters and settlers. (We won't dwell on the fact that many of the Cheyenne and Sioux warriors who fought Custer at the Little Big Horn in 1876 were armed with '73s, in some cases, badly outgunning the doomed soldiers who carried out-dated, single-shot military carbines.)

For men of means, having their photographs taken in a professional studio after the hunt was a popular endeavor that brought them much status among their peers. Photo circa late 1880s.

LEARNING FROM OUR INDIAN BROTHERS

This 1837 French engraving set in Spanish Florida by Traversier Arnout depicts an Eastern Indian using a deer skin to sneak within bow range of his quarry. A century later, innovative American deer hunters like Howard Hill and Fred Bear were learning how to hunt deer and other big game with longbows and homemade arrowheads. It didn't take long before American ingenuity created a plethora of modern bow hunting equipment.

"LEATHER STOCKINGS."

This 1891 stereoview by B.W. Kilburn of Littleton, New Hampshire shows a bearded veteran hunter holding a rabbit-eared, double-barreled, percussion shotgun as he looks over his hard-won bounty. It's a cold day in the New England woods; the snow is deep but he has his venison. He appears to be wearing homemade leggings. A snow-covered cabin is barely visible in the background. This old-timer could well have been one of the defenders of Cemetery Ridge at Gettysburg nearly 30 years earlier.

"A PRONOUNCED CASE OF BUCK FEVER"
The black powder muzzleloader sends a cloud of smoke over the head of the young forkhorn hidden on the bank of the lake as the hunter in the canoe is stricken with a case of buck fever. Companies like B.W. Kilburn loved to "ham it up" in the late 1800s with fake scenes like this. Do you suppose anyone actually fell for it? Stereoview by B.W. Kilburn, Littleton, NH, circa 1893.

SUPPER TIME
With one fine buck and one ruffed grouse hanging in camp, this northwoods guide is preparing supper while his "sports" relax and smoke their pipes. A.B. Frost print, 1904.

"A HOME IN THE WOODS. ADIRONDACKS."

With several deer hanging in camp, these veteran hunters are lazing away a pleasant afternoon at their "home away from home" deep in the mountains. Supper will soon be sizzling in the frying pans and the aroma of grilled venison will fill the air. Throughout the last half of the 19th century, the Adirondack region became a destination for thousands of deer hunters and fishermen who ran the gambit on the economic ladder. Elaborate lodges were built for the very wealthy sportsmen who hailed from the cities, and hundreds of rustic camps like this one served the everyday sportsman who came from near and far to challenge the wilderness. Stereoview circa 1890.

"HAPPY HUNTERS HOMEWARD BOUND."

After an exhilarating day in the field that produced two fine deer, these snow-weary hunters are glad to be nearing the warm cabin. The man in the front is holding a half-magazine Winchester Model 1892 that has a 24-inch octagon barrel. Stereoview photo circa 1899.

A CORNUCOPIA OF VENISON

If the three seated ladies are impressed with the seemingly super-strength antics of the men-folk as they manhandle the carcasses of four deer, they certainly are not letting on. Stoic as they may seem in posing for the photo, the ladies have to be rejoicing at all of that prime venison.

It might be an unusual way to show off one's bounty, but deer hunters will do strange things to impress the womenfolk, especially when a camera is present. The budding deer hunter sitting in the foreground seems quite content to be posing with the 1894 Winchester lever-action rifle. Maybe it will be his someday. Photo circa 1898.

"SHOT IN A VITAL SPOT."

The day's hunt is over, the Winchesters are unloaded and now it's time to brag about that incredible shot. Since times immemorial, hunters have gathered together after the hunt to relive the moment and talk about shots made, shots missed and other exciting events of the day. Stereoview circa 1885.

HUNTING WITH HOUNDS IN THE WILDS OF CANADA
A bevy of side-by-side shotguns with rabbit ears and a sagging meat pole indicates these proud Canadians and their fine-looking hounds have done a good day's work in the deer woods. The pair of 1872 Winchester lever-action repeaters no doubt came in handy for some of the longer shots. These men certainly know how to celebrate the finer aspects of life. Photo courtesy of Bill Cooper, circa 1890.

A STROKE OF GENIUS
Since this proud hunter is grasping a tine from the handsome 10-pointer, is he trying to tell us this outstanding trophy is his? Could all three bucks be the result of his handiwork? It's entirely possible since these deer were killed at a time when very few hunting regulations or bag limits existed. If so, our charmed hunter must be equally proud of his beautifully balanced Winchester 1886 lever-action rifle, compliments of the gun-making genius of John M. Browning. The round-barrel, half-magazine takedown frame with an uncheckered pistol grip stock was originally chambered in .45-70, .45-90 WCF and .40-82 WCF and designed for conventional black powder. Because of its strongly constructed action, it easily converted to smokeless powder in later years, with only minor modifications. Beginning in 1903, it was chambered for the .33 WCF. The barrel came in a variety of lengths, ranging from 22 to 28 inches. Photo circa 1905.

LAST OF THE CARIBOU

These successful hunters obviously are serious about their sport. To have one's trophy whitetail or caribou head mounted by a competent taxidermist in the late 1800s was anything but common. It is unknown whether or not these trophy heads were taken in southern Ontario or along the northern edges of the Upper Midwest or northern Maine where caribou were once fairly abundant. During the late 1800s, and into the early 1900s, American sportsmen, including Theodore Roosevelt, hunted caribou on both sides of the border. With one long-barreled Winchester 1873 lever-action rifle (on far right), three others with round barrels and half magazines, and one sure-shooting Remington Model 1867 rolling block rifle, the men pictured here are no doubt seasoned hunters.

Before settlement, woodland caribou were native to much of northern Minnesota, northern Wisconsin and Upper Michigan. Numbers declined dramatically after the first settlers arrived. Unlike moose or deer, caribou were relatively easy to kill, and hunters could wipe out small herds with little effort. By the late 1800s, only a few remnant animals remained in isolated pockets near the Canadian border. One of the last caribou was killed on Isle Royale in Lake Superior in 1929. Likewise, caribou were also native to much of Maine, but indiscriminate hunting in the late 1800s took its toll. Caribou hunting was banned in Maine in 1899. Attempts were made to restore caribou in northern Maine in the early 20th century, but predators and poaching ended all hopes of restoring this once noble deer. Photo circa 1895.

"OUR CHRISTMAS HUNT, 1893."

The dogs have done their job, and plenty of mouth-watering roast venison will be consumed on Christmas Day. The hunter on the left is holding a Marlin Model 1893, while the long barreled lever-action repeater held by the man on the right appears to be a Marlin '92. Section from a stereoview by B.W. Kilburn, circa 1893.

THE MARKET HUNTERS

As mentioned in the introduction, market hunting throughout the 19th century was responsible for depleting vast numbers of fish and wildlife across the country. Some species, like passenger pigeons, were hunted to extinction. Whitetails were hunted for their skins and meat and, by 1900, their numbers had fallen to all-time lows in the U.S. Hunting seasons and bag limits were eventually established in each state. Although wildlife management became an exciting new science in the early 1900s, little money was available to put sound conservation strategies into practice.

Thanks to American sportsmen, namely deer hunters, an excise tax on the sale of firearms and ammunition provided funds for states to pay for wildlife management and habitat protection. With the passing of the Pittman-Robertson Act in 1936, the age of real scientific wildlife management was born. However, the program did not see much daylight until after World War II. To date, billions of sportsmens' tax dollars have been funneled into various wildlife programs.

MARKET HUNTERS IN THE DEEP SOUTH
These hunters and their dogs have taken plenty of game; turkeys, deer and possibly a wild hog or two. With several drying deer skins and plenty of hanging meat, these market hunters likely are operating in central Florida. Heavy market hunting in the late 1800s and early 1900s took its toll on Florida's deer and turkey populations. By the late 1930s, less than 30,000 deer remained in the state. Then, just when things couldn't get much worse, an effort by the state to eradicate the cattle-fever tick from 1939 to 1941 claimed another 10,000 deer in South Florida. Thanks to a successful restocking program by the Florida Game and Fresh Water Fish Commission that gained momentum after the war, whitetails purchased from out of state sources (including a game farm in Wisconsin) were transplanted to areas where deer numbers were low. Photos circa 1910.

AN INSATIABLE DEMAND
Tagged and ready to be shipped out by rail from Mackinaw, Michigan, this amazing mountain of venison from the northern tip of Lower Peninsula (with one huge bruin on top of the pile and possibly a smaller bear on the far left) is probably going directly to a large city to the south like Grand Rapids or Lansing. There it will wind up in butcher shops, hotel restaurants and other big-city eateries. Supplying an insatiable demand for venison at the turn of the century was a never-ending job, but plenty of eager young men who became market hunters were on hand to fill that need. Several outstanding racks can be seen among the heap of carcasses. Photo circa early 1900s.

NORTHEAST MARKET HUNTERS
Judging by the ages of the deer hanging in camp, the rifles and the demeanor of this rough and tumble group, it's probably a safe bet to assume these men are market hunters operating somewhere in the northeast—northern Pennsylvania, New York State or possibly New England. Looks like at least two Winchester 1895s and one Model '94 were responsible for bringing down most of the deer. With few game laws in the East in the late 1800s and a large demand for venison in cities like New York and Boston, these seasoned hunters could make good money selling venison. Note the covered wagon in the background. Photo circa late 1890s.

"Take dur (deer), now. A little young dur is purty an' sweet. But hit grows to a buck with antlers. An', come fall, hits neck swells turrible, an' hit's all in a franzy to get hitself a she-un, an' chargin' other males to fit (fight) to the death. Hit mebbe follered ye around, gentle as a calf, all summer. But come fall, hit'll go ye, an' strike ye down with hits forefeet, jest like ye was a enemy.

". . . humans is humans an' critters is critters; an' the critters, too, has got their own kind of self-respect an' their own laws an' ways of livin'. Wild is wild."

Cecile Hulse Matschat
Suwanee River – Strange Green Land (1938)

THE SPOILS OF A DAY'S HUNT

Taken in Whitefish, Montana, in 1902, this old photo could have come directly from a scene in the blockbuster movie *Lonesome Dove* based on Larry McMurtry's Pulitzer Prize winning novel. The distinguished hunter driving the wagon certainly bears a strong resemblance to the film version character, Captain W.F. Call, Texas Ranger, played by the ever-popular Tommy Lee Jones. The photo was actually taken about 20 years after the fictitious *Lonesome Dove* crew trailed their herd from South Texas to Montana Territory in the late 1870s.

Whoever he is, this lucky hunter and his companions apparently enjoyed some fine hunting in the mountains of western Montana. Could anyone back then have known that 100 years later, in the early 2000s, this same area would still be a prime whitetail destination, and that hunters from across the U.S. would travel to magical places like Big Fork, Whitefish and the Milk River to chase Montana whitetails like the beautiful five-by-five in the center of the wagon?

In addition to the three bucks, the wagon appears to be loaded with camp gear and several skins. Perhaps this man is a trapper/hunter bringing his bounty to market. What could be a heavy buffalo robe is draped over the three deer, not an uncommon sight across America in those days. After the slaughter of millions of bison, buffalo robes and ankle-length coats were quite the style after the turn of the century. In fact, they were a common winter sight in many eastern population centers, especially in such "tame" places as New York City!

Note: This is one of several photos in this book that previously appeared in Volume I of *Dawn of American Deer Hunting*. Because the photo originally appeared with no caption, I decided to run it again with its very interesting caption.

CHAPTER 2

THE GILDED AGE OF WHITETAIL HUNTING (EARLY 1900s)

The Gilded Age in America was a 30-year period of rapid growth, expansion and industrialization that took place from the end of the Civil War to the beginning of the new century. The term was first used by Mark Twain and Charles Dudley Warner in their classic 1873 novel, *The Gilded Age: A Tale of Today*, in which they satirized the idea of "get rich quick schemes" through land speculations that were so prevalent in the early 1870s.

To the authors' way of thinking, "a thin gilding of gold" was something artificial that represented the mythical idea of getting rich quickly through speculation. In truth, speculation often led to disaster.

On a national scale, the Gilded Age did in fact represent a time like never before. Due to the country's rapid industrial growth, incredible wealth was attained by families, individuals and companies through the commercial expansion of such important new industries as oil, steel and transportation. But it came with a price. Along with that rapid growth and westward expansion, the country also experienced wanton exploitation of its natural resources. By the turn of the century, people began to realize that abundant resources once thought to be limitless might disappear forever.

By the early 1880s, millions of buffalo had been slaughtered on the western plains in less than two decades, putting the species on the brink of extinction. By 1900, millions of passenger pigeons had disappeared from eastern forests. White-tailed deer and wild turkeys rapidly declined in many eastern states as a result of market hunting and the deerhide trade. Virgin timber began to disappear in the Northeast, the Southeast and the Upper Midwest, leaving tens of thousands of acres of cutover wasteland. The mining of gold and other valuable minerals created erosion on mountainsides and silt pollution in streams and rivers. The old adage that a gray squirrel could climb a tree on the East Coast and work its way to the West coast without ever touching the ground was no longer valid.

To America's credit, visionary leaders like President Theodore Roosevelt began to take vital steps to protect, restore and preserve precious resources. Game laws were established and enforced in many states. Wildlife refuges and sanctuaries were established to protect fish and wildlife species. For the first time ever, wildlife resources were looked upon as renewable, but certainly not limitless.

If there ever was a gilded age of whitetail hunting in America, it occurred in the first two decades of the 20th century. New innovations in firearms, carried over from the late 1800s, continued to benefit sport hunters. For the first time in history, gun manufacturers like Remington, Winchester, Marlin and Savage were producing non-military rifles, shotguns, bullets and equipment specifically made for hunters.

New modes of transportation—namely automobiles and railroads—made it possible for hunters to become more mobile than ever before. Hunters could now travel to distant and hard-to-reach destinations once difficult and time-consuming to reach with a horse and wagon. In some areas like northern Maine, short-line railroads were built specifically to transport sportsmen from cities to remote hunting and fishing camps.

The new century saw almost two full decades of peacetime with no devastating wars to plague the growing nation, making it easier for whitetail hunters to focus their efforts on America's No. 1 big game animal. Sadly, all that changed in 1917 when thousands of American boys were sent to the muddy and rat-infested trenches in France.

Whitetail hunting in America was always influenced by our ancestors. European immigrants from countries like Germany, Russia, Italy, Norway and Sweden had poured into the U.S. in the late 1800s. Having settled in Midwestern states like Minnesota, Wisconsin and Michigan, it didn't take long before these ethnic groups were participating in that purely American ritual of going to deer camp each autumn. To these groups, whitetail hunting would become important generational traditions. In short, you might say the early 20th century was a gold-plated time for many American and immigrant-American deer hunters. Indeed it was the "gilded age" of whitetail hunting!

1903 advertisement promoting the revolutionary new "smokeless" .38-55 cartridge for the Marlin repeater.

ADIRONDACK CAMP HUNTING SEASON
The all-knowing guide stands with his hands on his hips as the "sports" on the right pose in front of the cabin. The older gentleman has a Remington Model 8 while the younger man to his right holds a Savage '99. Several Winchesters lean against the cabin wall. The young man behind the older gentleman is holding something in his hand, possibly a cartridge casing that brought down one of the deer. Photo circa 1910.

ROUGH AND READY
Judging from the variety of popular deer rifles these roughhewn hunters are holding, it's little wonder this rugged northwoods group has managed to weigh down the meat pole. The hunter on the far left has a Winchester Model '07, while the bearded man next to him sports a lever-action rifle. The hunter third from the left has a Winchester 1895, while the man next him also holds a lever action. The older gent second from the right has a side-by-side that appears to be a Remington Model 1889 12 gauge, while the younger man next to him holds a rifle that cannot be identified. Photo circa 1914.

SAGES OF DEER CAMP

This photo depicts two old veterans of many hunting camps posing with their highly-prized rifles. Could the two gentlemen be Civil War veterans as well? The white-bearded hunter on the left is holding an 1893 Marlin, marketed by that company as a "Rifle for Big Game." Offered in .30-30, .32-40 and .38-55 calibers, a vintage Marlin ad that ran a few years after this photo was taken in 1918 promoted the popular '93s as "Quick Handling, Powerful, Accurate Guns. Built in Perfect Proportion Throughout . . ." The high-power smokeless loads were "Ideal for Shooting Bear, Moose, Deer and All American Big Game." Prices in 1918 ranged from $24 to $32. Photo circa 1910.

ADMIRING THE TROPHY

Two of the younger hunters in camp show off the spoils of the day. The man on the right holds a Winchester Model 1895. Used as both a military and sporting rifle, the '95 was the first Winchester rifle to feature a box magazine. This enabled it to safely handle and chamber spitzer bullets. It was the last lever-action rifle to be designed by John Browning. Popular sporting loads included the .30-03, .30 Army, .30-06, .35 Winchester, .38-72 Winchester, .40-72 Winchester and .405 Winchester. Photo circa 1910.

A group photo showing some of the other camp members. All three cabinet photos are believed to be from the Upper Midwest, circa 1910.

WARM-GLOWING CAMARADERIE

This weathered photo shows four hunters in front of their cabin with an assortment of lever-action rifles, mostly Winchesters. At right, the old gentleman shows off a very nice buck. He's holding an original Model 95 Winchester. Photos circa 1910.

LURE OF THE WILD

Wielding a short-barreled Winchester Model 94 "trapper's carbine" and a pair of Savage 99s, these well-heeled city sports won't soon forget the memorable time spent afield or the outstanding eight-pointer that fell to one of their rifles. Although the postcard rack is the real attention getter, the smaller buck on the ground is also a well-earned prize for the lucky huntsman who brought it down. Photo circa 1910.

EVERYONE SHOULD HAVE A GRANDFATHER LIKE THIS

You can see the pride on Gramps' face—both for the hefty fork-horn buck that he downed with his trusty '95 Winchester as well as for his rifle-wielding grandson who is one lucky lad. The boy no doubt worships his grandpa. He's holding a Hamilton Model 27 .22 caliber singe-shot, a breakdown rifle with a 16-inch barrel, probably a gift from Gramps. The Model 27 was first introduced in 1907 and was often referred to as the "quintessential boy's rifle." Production ceased in 1930. Prior to World War I, the Model 27 could be bought out of the Sears Roebuck catalog for $1.50 to $2. After the war, it was advertised at a whopping $2.55. The Hamilton Rifle Co. was established in Plymouth, Michigan in 1898 by Clarence J. Hamilton, a brilliant gunsmith, and his son, Coella. The company ended production in 1945. Photo circa 1910.

SPRINGTIME PURSUIT

You know the lady of the house has to be proud of her man. Wielding his trusty Marlin Model 1893 lever-action with a tang sight, that fat doe will provide some mighty good eatings. This deer might have been killed at a time and place where no set seasons yet existed as the prairie flowers indicate the season as mid-spring. Photo circa early 1900s.

CAMP GOOD LUCK

Lord a mercy! The happy souls in Camp Good Luck had to erect another meat pole just to hold all of their venison. Those horseshoes above the tent flap must have performed some special magic. The men are wielding an assortment of long guns, including several shotguns and a bevy of fancy Winchester and Marlin lever-actions. The fourth man from the left appears to be holding a Marlin 1895 carbine, but the other lever guns are difficult to identify. Let's hope some of these hunters didn't run out of bullets. Camp Good Luck certainly has lived up to its namesake. The camp cook may have bitten off more than he can chew. Photo circa 1900.

GLORY DAYS IN NORTHERN MAINE
These well-armed men have good reason to be grinning. Three of the hunters are holding Remington Model 8s, one has a shotgun and four others are brandishing 1894 Winchesters. The man second from the left is holding a Winchester Model 94 half-round, half-octagon with a smooth stock. The man next to him also has a '94 Winchester with a half magazine—half-round, half-octagon, but his rifle has a pistol-grip stock and tang sights. The other two Winchesters are '94 carbines. Photo circa 1905.

COZY WISCONSIN DEER CAMP
Posed with their long-barreled Winchester Model 94 rifles and a meat pole straining with beefy young bucks, these stoic hunters may well be members of the same family so typical of many of the groups of European immigrants who settled in the Upper Midwest and began a cherished tradition of spending a week or two in deer camp every season. The forest around them appears to have been recently timbered. The ladies are probably wives who have come to help with the cooking. These hard-working immigrants hunted for both food and enjoyment, and their yearly pilgrimages to the deer woods would come to span many generations. Photo circa 1900.

"EACH HUNTER SECURED HIS REWARD."
With four deer hanging, it's time to relax and reflect on a perfect day in the woods. The hunter on the right is holding a Marlin 1893 lever-action repeater. The rifle leaning against the tree belonging to the young man in the foreground could be a Remington rolling block. Stereoview circa 1906.

A GOOD DAY'S WORK
The older man on the left could be the father of one or both of the younger hunters in the foreground. The shotgun held by the young man on the right is a Winchester Model 1887 12-gauge with a 30-inch barrel. Notice his belt filled with shells, probably smokeless. The Model '87 was the precursor to a long line of repeating shotguns that would follow in the new century. The man in the center has a Marlin 1893 repeater, while the man on the left holds a gun that has all the earmarks of being a Winchester Model 1897 pump action 16-gauge shotgun. The Model '97 was a more modern version of the Model '93. Over one million of these shotguns were produced from 1897 to 1957. The '97 was available in numerous grades and could be bought as a solid frame or takedown. It was chambered in 12 and 16 gauge. Photo circa 1905.

A MOVABLE FEAST

It's unlikely these businessmen are the actual hunters responsible for bagging this carload of bucks, but they seem to be enjoying themselves nonetheless as they pose for the camera. The automobile appears to be a 1917 or 1918 vintage Monroe roadster "light car." Apparently, it's just what the doctor ordered for transporting at least five hefty bucks from the field to the ice house. Photo circa 1920.

GAME-GETTING SHOTGUN

This young man must be extremely proud of his eight-point buck. He's gone to great lengths to stake it up in the snow and show off the single-shot Iver Johnson "Champion" 16-gauge shotgun responsible for the deed. Long considered the common man's shotgun, Iver Johnsons were well made and dependable. They brought down plenty of game, especially squirrels, rabbits and quail. This single-shot hammer model was probably made in the early 1900s and used smokeless shells. Photo circa 1908.

"HANGING DEER – 'NOW GUIDE, A MOOSE BEFORE NIGHTFALL.'"
The hunter and his guide have a fine buck to hang up. Stereoview by Keystone View Company, circa 1898.

"GUIDE PACKING IN THE DAY'S CATCH."
The "sport" follows as his guide carries the day's bounty back to camp. Written on the back of this stereoview was: "Sportsmen find their vivacity at the highest pitch as they pursue their game in forest and mountain. The true huntsman does not kill for mere slaughter; he rebukes the butcher of game who does. The sportsman kills for necessary food or because of the nerve and daring and enterprise of the sport." Steroview by Keystone View Company, circa 1901.

SEIZING THE DAY

A tall meat pole filled with deer, one small bear and a furry critter that could be a bobcat taken by an array of fine weapons bares proof this proud group has shared a special camaraderie in their deer camp near Gemfask, Michigan. The older gentleman on the right cradles a fine double gun possibly brought over from the old country, while the white-bearded man to his right leans on his well-used Marlin Model 1893. The man in the middle proudly holds a Winchester Model 1897 pump 12-gauge shotgun. The hunter on the far left has a Savage 99 while the two men in front of him have lever-action rifles. By the contented looks on their faces, the men in this ethnic group (could they be of German or Swedish descent?), wouldn't trade places with the Czar of Russia.
Photo circa 1910.

BORN TO HUNT

These seasoned hunters seem to be as proud of their Model 1907 Winchester self-loading rifles as they are of their swollen-necked prize. The .351 High Power cartridge used in the '07 delivered a 130-grain bullet that apparently did a more-than-adequate job on this hefty old mossback.
Photo circa 1915.

"I think the reason I have always loved the sport of deer hunting so much lies in its inherent challenge, for the whitetail is the smartest creature to walk this earth. It has eyes for anything that makes the slightest movement, and it has a nose that can pick up just about any scent, and it has ears that act like radar, warning it of any sound that is out of place. To outwit a creature as well-tuned to its environment as the whitetail takes some doing . . ."

Fred Bear
From *Deer and Deer Hunting*
By Dr. Rob Wegner (1984)

HUNTER'S PARADISE

Hailing from their cozy deer camp in northern Maine's Aroostook County, these proud hunters display a fine array of deer along with several mouth-watering grouse. Throughout most of the 20th century, Aroostook County, nestled in the shadow of Mt. Katahdin, was a prime destination for hunters and fly fisherman, offering deer, bear and moose as well as unparalleled trout fishing. Photo circa 1938.

CHAPTER 3

DREAMS, DUST AND HARD WORK: THE MAGIC OF DEER CAMP

Nothing brings men more closely together than the rough and crude atmosphere of deer camp. For generations, fathers, sons, grandsons, wives, daughters, uncles and good friends have spent the blistering months of July and August dreaming about November, preparing gear, counting the days until that magic date appears on the calendar—Opening Day! Then and only then do they truly come alive in a special way. They whistle, they sing and they smile as they reach in the closet and unzip the worn old rifle case and apply a coat of oil to that soon-to-be classic Savage 99, Remington Model 8 or Winchester 1895. Life is good!

Soon it will be time to pack the gear and the food, hike back to the old cabin, check the roof for leaks and once again stake a claim for the always-too-short deer season. Any rats or mice that have taken up residence in the cabin will have to be dealt with, and it might be a real challenge to figure out how to get that stubborn old skunk out from underneath the cabin without getting sprayed. The meat pole outside will have to be reinforced or maybe even extended; after all, according to the almanac, the weather is going to be prime for rutting bucks.

Somewhere, a 12-year-old boy will be allowed to hunt by himself for the first time, and he'll be using Grandpa's weathered old Savage 99. Someday, that beloved rifle will be his. When that day comes, no prince in line to inherit a vast kingdom could be gaining more wealth, because the true value of some earthly objects can only be measured by what lives in the heart. The impact and joy of receiving an heirloom rifle handed down from grandfather to father to son cannot be measured in dollars and cents.

Yesteryear's deer camps came in all sizes and descriptions; from the most elaborate and luxurious lodges in the Adirondacks and northern Maine catering to wealthy clients from the city to well-maintained log cabins used several times a year by family members or ethnic groups. Countless primitive and rustic deer shacks, some barely large enough to hold two men, peppered the wilderness and served their occupants well if only for a day or two when deer season finally arrived.

Tent camping was also vastly popular. Large store-bought canvas wall tents equipped with wood-burning stoves served groups of four to six hunters, while smaller two-man tents fit the bill for hunters who were constantly on the move. For the real trailblazers who enjoyed being in the elements and living close to nature, lean-tos and temporary shelters made from brush and limbs with a good fire pit kept one warm and dry at night.

With the advent of short-line railroads in many states and the newfangled automobile starting to see heavy use in the early 1900s, yesteryear's hunters instantly became more mobile than ever before. For the first time ever, destinations across the state or even out of state could be reached in much less time, making it possible to reach new and prime whitetail country never before so easily accessible.

Hunters could go to deer camp for a couple of days or a couple of weeks. Much like today, those hunters lucky enough to live on farms or out in the hinterlands could step out the back door and be in the whitetail deer woods in a matter of minutes.

No matter what kind of accommodations a man might have, once he reached deer camp, he became king of his own destiny. Deer camp was always a magical place. Even though the quarry was never easy to bring down, dreams, dust and hard work usually helped tip the scales in the hunter's favor.

CAREFUL WHERE YOU STEP

A long, makeshift stretcher seems to be just what these hunters need to manhandle their heavy buck out of the woods and back to camp. The fine buck has at least six points on its left antler and four or five on the right. Photo circa 1930s.

WHEN MEN WERE MEN
 These three lucky hunters have managed to accumulate enough venison to last most of the winter, but they are certainly getting their spoils out of the woods the hard way. All three deer appear to be does, although the smaller deer on the right could be a young buck. Interestingly, the rifle carried by the man in front is a Savage Arms Model 1920 Hi-Power, probably in .250-3000 caliber. This well made, lightweight sporting rifle was the company's first attempt to produce a bolt-action firearm. It originally came in .250-3000 caliber, and later was offered in the popular .300 Savage. Sadly, its production life was short— from 1920 to 1928. Photo circa 1925.

CABIN BLUFF
 Howard Coffin (second from left), owner of Cabin Bluff Resort in southeast Georgia, and President Calvin Coolidge (1872-1933, second from right) pose happily after a successful day's hunt. Their bag includes several turkeys and pheasants and one deer. Vice President Coolidge was elevated to the presidency in 1923 upon the death of Warren G. Harding while in office. Elected to a full term in 1924, he served as the 30th president of the United States. Coolidge is best known for restoring integrity to the executive office after a number of scandals rocked the previous administration. An avid hunter and fisherman, this photo was taken in the late 1920s after Coolidge left office. Sadly, he died from a heart attack in 1933 at the relatively young age of 60.

SWEET NOVEMBER
Sporting several Savage 99s and shotguns, these Pennsylvania hunters have managed to return from the day's hunt with plenty of prime venison to divvy up. With several inches of snow on the ground, November 1926 was an ideal time to be in the woods.

MEAT ON THE MOVE
These four young men appear to be very happy with the big doe one of them shot. The two toting the doe appear to be carrying Winchesters. The hunter in the foreground is toting a long-barreled Winchester, while his partner is carrying an older model. Photo circa 1910.

FIRE PREVENTION AND DETECTION IN THE ADIRONDACKS

Avid whitetail hunter and woodsman Louis J. Fagan (1886-1974) of Gloverville, New York built one of the first fire towers in the Adirondacks. After several devastating fires in 1903 and 1908 that burned almost one million acres of forestland, New York State developed an intensive fire prevention and containment program. The first tower was built on top of Mount Morris in 1909. Several others were built in nearby areas. Fagan and his crew were commissioned to build a wooden tower on top of Cathead Mountain near Big Tupper Lake in Hamilton County. The tower was constructed in 1910.

Upon completion of the Cathead Mountain fire tower in 1910, Fagan and Percy Cole proudly erected an American flag atop the observation deck. Within a year or two, enclosed shelters were built atop the deck so observers would have better protection from the harsh elements as they searched the horizon for smoke.

Louis Fagan (second from right) poses at the base of Cathead Tower next to the small cabin the men stayed in while they erected the structure.

Louis Fagan, an avid hunter who sometimes was known as "The Old Man of the Mountain," stands on the left as his hunting party poses with a number of fine bucks and several bears. Photo circa 1917. All photos courtesy of Carol Appleton, great granddaughter of Louis J. Fagan.

SOMEWHERE IN THE EASTERN MOUNTAINS
Decked out in his leather leggings and carrying a Winchester Model 1907 .351 highpower takedown, this well-dressed and triumphant hunter is packing out his deer skin and head by horseback. Perhaps he already collected the meat earlier. Photo circa 1915.

A FEAST IN THE MAKING
The snowshoes are leaning against the tent and the rifles have been retired for the evening. Preparing to cook a deer shoulder over the open fire, the hunters in this camp will eat well tonight! Photo circa 1910.

MILLBRIDGE CLUB
These shotgunners belonged to the Millbridge Deer Hunting Club in Millbridge, New Jersey. Millbridge is located 10 miles northeast of Philadelphia not far from the Delaware River. During the early years of the Great Depression, the first-class duck hunting was an added bonus to the excellent deer hunting.

DREAMS, DUST AND HARD WORK: THE MAGIC OF DEER CAMP

"CAMP SCENE—HANGING UP THE BIG BEAR."
Heave Ho! It takes a lot of muscle to hoist this big bruin off the ground in deer camp. Although these rugged hunters are no doubt primarily after whitetails, no one is going to pass up a chance at a big bear. Several lever-action rifles are leaning against the logs, one being a Winchester Model 1873, and a black-powder shotgun rests next to the Winchester. Stereoview by Underwood and Underwood, circa 1893.

DEEP IN THE NORTH WOODS
This early scene of a north woods hunting camp shows one of the members rustling up the evening's repast while his buddies are out searching for more deer to add to the meat pole, which is already bending under the weight of several whitetails and two black bears.

DIAMONDBACK COUNTRY
Western diamondbacks and gnarly whitetails seem to go together in South Texas. In the photo at left is a young hunter who is taking no chances. Wearing snake leggings and holding his trusty Marlin '93—likely a .30-30—he's found some good hunting in the brush country with at least one of these deer. The other photo shows his companion wielding a beautifully checkered Winchester 1905 self-loading semi-automatic. Despite the pesky snakes, the pair found good hunting. Photo circa 1915.

BUCKSHOT AND BUCK FEVER
It's a cold snowy day near Owensville, Missouri and a good buck is finally down. Judging by the looks on their faces, each of these men had a hand in the hunt. Were they executing a drive? Did one of the drivers jump this buck as he was bedded in the snow? Did the crafty buck run by one of the standers? Three of the men have shotguns, two have rifles. The details of the story have been lost to time, but the memory will be etched in the hearts of these men for all time. Photo postcard circa 1910.

TROUT IN THE MORNING, QUAIL IN THE AFTERNOON
With shotguns in hand, Howard and Matilda Coffin, owners of the famed Cabin Bluff Resort in southeast Georgia, pose at the barbeque pits near the Cumberland River. Apparently they are headed to the quail coverts after catching a mess of trout and one hefty largemouth bass. Photo circa 1932.

ABOUT CABIN BLUFF RESORT
Hudson Auto pioneer Howard E. Coffin established the 11,000-acre Cabin Bluff Resort in 1928 as a world-class hunting and fishing destination for wealthy businessmen and outdoorsmen. The land is located in Southeast Georgia just across the intracoastal waterway from Cumberland Island National Seashore.

Prior to the Civil War, the Floyd family prospered by growing Sea Island cotton on the property. The Floyds had also established the Camden Hunt Club in 1827, one of the first clubs of its kind in the nation to serve wealthy sportsmen. After the Civil War, the cotton industry was slow to recover and much of the land reverted back to nature. Heavy logging occurred in the early 1900s until Howard Coffin purchased the tract in 1927. He envisioned Cabin Bluff as a perfect hunting and outdoor retreat for the wealthy.

During the ensuing years, Cabin Bluff hosted presidents, successful businessmen and distinguished sporting enthusiasts from around the world.

In June 2018, a total of 11,172 acres of the Cabin Bluff property was purchased by the Nature Conservancy. Long-term plans include protecting the extensive longleaf pine forests and rare plants and animals such as the gopher tortoise, which is currently listed as a threatened species. The resort operations are expected to continue through a partnership agreement with an outside party.

THE PICTURE OF CONTENTMENT

With Winchester in hand and pipe in mouth, this proud hunter has done his day's work. Now he can take off his boots, sit back and reflect about those delicious backstraps that will soon be sizzling over the fire as he relaxes in his newfangled "camp body," an early version of a mobile truck camper shell. Ah, Life in the deer woods is good! Photo circa 1925.

A MAN AND HIS RIFLE

The sweet-shooting Remington Model 8 auto has once again proved its worth, and this proud young hunter couldn't be more satisfied. With a good buck on the ground and a fine rifle that has performed flawlessly in the woods, what more could a dedicated young outdoorsman hope for? Photo circa 1915.

"Now is the Moon of the Rutting Stag, as the Indians used to say, and in the cool of the morning, if he's lucky, a hunter can step out on the back porch of his cabin and hear the big bucks blowing and whistling over a distant ridge top. And sometimes, way up toward the slopes of Blood or Slaughter mountains, he can see laurel thrashing where they fight."

Harold Martin, from a column
in the *Atlanta Constitution*, Oct. 20, 1944

NORTH COUNTRY GIANTS
Lots of Winchesters and a Marlin or two were responsible for several crackerjack bucks and one small bear cub, probably taken in northern Minnesota or Wisconsin. Most of these men are likely recent immigrants whose families made their way to the Midwest and began the respected tradition of hunting together each November. Photo circa 1905.

CHAPTER 4

MOON OF THE RUTTING STAG

Harold Martin captured the true essence of the autumn rutting season as he went on to say, "When the mast is heavy the deer will stay fat and sleek all winter on the acorns, and the bear, who are his friends, will lie cradled in rolls of fat, and the wild hogs will have some meat on their ribs, and all of the people of the woods will come into spring fat and sassy.

". . . A heavy mast means that when spring clothes the hills in green again, the fawns will be strong and healthy and nimble on their thin legs as they flash their little flags from the windfalls and the streams. And the yearling bucks will be husky and strong as they grow into spike-horn stags."

Come fall, those spike-horn stags will be feeling their oats. They may stay out of the way of the big boys, and they don't quite know what to do with their bulging muscles and raging hormones, but they learn quickly enough and they try to act out the part in every way—making scrapes, thrashing shrubs with their tiny antlers, chasing and irritating does, engaging in pushing and shoving contests with other yearlings and, in general, trying to be the bad boys of the neighborhood.

Since times immemorial, hunters have known the rutting season is the best time to be in the woods. The term, "the Moon of the Rutting Stag" comes directly from the Cherokee Indians. If the mast was unusually good, those thick-necked bucks seemingly had limitless energy as they searched the woods for receptive does. This was one of the few times when a crafty old mossback was apt to slip up and get caught an hour after daylight as he searched the woods for a mate. And in his zeal to corner an elusive doe, a buck might let down his guard and present a shot to a patient hunter.

In his 1972 book *The Whitetail Deer Guide*, author Ken Heuser wrote, "When you see a buck traveling along with his nose to the ground and his tail straight out back, he's trailing a doe. This is the time a buck can get so excited he will hop stiff legged, looking at the brush and grunting at every hop. His eyes will become glassy and often he will stand with his hindquarters sagging. The buck's odor becomes very strong at this time. A trained human nose will pick it up at quite a distance. I have smelled them at close to 100 yards away when I was downwind. The strong odor comes from the buck's metatarsal glands and from his wallowing in his scrape. Occasionally a buck will get so excited he will rub his shoulders in the mud of the scrape until they are well coated. It doesn't take too long before the old boy smells worse than the elephant pit at the zoo."

Few hunters of yesteryear specifically hunted the rut or targeted individual bucks, but they certainly recognized the unmistakable smell of musk. And just like it does today, that rank smell that sometimes lingered in the wet morning woods got their blood "to boiling." Most turn-of-the-century hunters engaged in some type of group hunting. Some were still-hunters and some were stand-hunters, but as a general rule, even lone hunters were opportunists who shot whatever they saw—buck or doe—while tracking or waiting patiently for whatever might happen by the stump they were sitting on.

The majority of hunters were well aware of the breeding season, but few considered it as the best time to shoot a buck. Most vintage hunters viewed cold weather and snow as the driving motivations for getting out in the woods, but the sight of a buck chasing a doe was always exhilarating. And since most hunting seasons occurred in November, the Moon of the Rutting Stag was always a magical time.

MUTUAL ADMIRATION SOCIETY
Several outstanding bucks hang on the meat pole as the relaxed hunters who shot them pose for the camera with their lever-action rifles. After corralling this many nice bucks in the cold and the snow, these men are no doubt feeling pretty good about their hunting abilities. Photo circa 1900.

DEER HUNTER'S VALHALLA
It's really not Viking heaven, but some of these hardy men might be related to Vikings. Several beautiful bucks hang on the meat pole in this sprawling camp. It appears as though the moon of the rutting stag has been very good to these diehard deer slayers. Lots of Winchester repeaters and at least one Savage '99 helped bring down this outlandish supply of venison. Photo circa 1906.

MR. WILSON'S PRIZE BUCK
Using his tried-and-true Winchester Model 94, Charles Wilson shot this fine eight-point buck in November 1937.

A BUCK IN THE BARN
This gentleman hunter is showing off the wide-spreading antlers of his buck. Photo circa 1930.

ONE FOR THE ROAD
If this outstanding Massachusetts heavyweight could talk, he would probably have an interesting story to tell. We don't know much about him, but the photo does reveal a somewhat swollen neck, indicating he was probably out chasing does when someone's well-paced bullet stopped him cold. The license tag reads "1955 Mass."

A REVOLUTIONARY RIFLE

This proud hunter took this outstanding buck with his revolutionary self-loading, six-shot, semiautomatic Winchester rifle. It appears to be the early '05 edition with a 22-inch barrel. It sold for about $25 in the early teens and came in .32 and .35 W.S.L. (self-loading) calibers. An extra magazine could be bought for about $1.50. The 1907 model was chambered for a heavier .351 S.L.R. cartridge and had a 10-shot magazine. Extremely popular with deer and big game hunters, it was also used by the Texas Rangers on the Mexican border in the early 1900s. Photo circa 1910.

GOOD HUNTING FOR THE WEES MEN

Postcard from Bon Echo Park, Ontario, Canada, (just North of Lake Ontario) with the written inscription: "First Day outing, Second day better, Wm. And J.S. Wees." (Date hard to read, may be "Nov. 1899." The man in front (could be the father) holds a Winchester 1873 lever-action while the man behind him (could be his son) carries a Marlin 1893 with an octagonal barrel. Photo circa 1899.

SPLIT BROWS
Perhaps it was an especially cool and quiet morning during the moon of the rutting stag when this feisty buck decided to let down his guard a wee bit and seek out a mate. The man in the checked wool jacket had other plans. Now that unusual rack with the split brow tines will adorn his wall for many years to come. Photo dated Nov. 17, 1954.

NOW THAT'S A DEER HUNTER
With his lace-up boots, hunting knife, bullet belt and trusty Remington Model 8, this hunter looks like he's been to the deer woods a few times. No matter how many fine bucks a hunter brings home, it's always a thrill to put another notch on the old rifle. Photo circa 1915.

A RARE AND UNFORGETTABLE DAY
Two fine bucks in one day. How often does that happen? Standing in the snow and holding a Winchester carbine across his arm, this charmed hunter will have plenty of venison to lay in for the winter. Photo circa 1920s.

HIS AND HERS

With two outstanding heavyweights on the hood of their 1927 or 1928 Dodge coup, it's hard to say whose buck is the largest. Maybe it should be a draw. For certain, this smiling couple apparently shared a day in the woods they'll not soon forget. Photo circa 1922.

REWARDS OF NOVEMBER

His Remington Model 8 has spoken and an elated hunter has his buck hanging back at camp. And what a fine buck it is! He and his trusty Model 8 have earned some bragging rights on this day. Looks like it's time to crank up the old Model T in the background and head back to civilization. The rewards of being in the deer woods are endless! Photo circa 1915.

BOB FINALLY GETS HIS DEER

What better way for a red-blooded, all-American outdoorsman to impress his lady friend than with a fine buck? In this picture postcard dated Nov. 19, 1908, Bob writes: "I've got my deer at last." The card is addressed to his sweetheart, Miss Sadie Roy of Walpole, New Hampshire. The gun appears to be a Remington Model 25 slide action. The buck appears to have been rutting heavily.

THE GLORY DAYS

These large-bodied bucks were probably taken during the rutting season at an upscale hunting lodge in the Adirondacks or northern Maine and were probably the result of a week's hunt. Meat poles like this were not uncommon at many hunting establishments in the early 1900s. Wonder if this contented hunter knows how fortunate he is to be living amidst such whitetail abundance... As he looks over the mountain of outstanding bucks, among them a young moose, he appears to be holding a Winchester Model 1894 rifle with a half-round, half-octagon barrel, probably made around 1905. Photo circa 1910.

SEASON OF DREAMS
Posed with his well-used Winchester Model 95, the hunter on the left has every reason to be pleased. So does his partner on the right, who is holding a Winchester '92 carbine and standing next to the large-bodied 10-pointer. Hunting near Grand Marais in Michigan's Upper Peninsula, these men have had an extraordinary few days. The boy sitting on the pole will never forget this moment. Photo circa 1907.

WHAT A RACK!
This Canisteo, New York hunter has every reason to be proud. Bucks of this quality don't step out in front of hunters every day. This old boy will no doubt find a place on the den wall. Photo 1965.

SAVAGE LAND
Bruiser bucks like this one don't make too many mistakes, and these two proud hunters know they have done a good day's work. Once again, a pair of Savage 99s ruled the day. Photo circa 1910, probably from the Upper Midwest.

COME NOVEMBER

Maybe the reason this quartet of redcoats is not all smiles is because they are still in shock about their incredible streak of success. Judging by some of these swollen-necked brutes, the timing of the rut must have been just right. Photo circa early 1950s.

DAD AND THE NOVEMBER GANG

With four bucks hanging, Dad and the gang have had another extraordinary year. From left are: John holding a Winchester Model 1895, Bud holding a military rifle (possibly an Argentine 1909 Mauser), Raymond holding a Remington Model 25 slide action, Dad with a Model 1892 Winchester carbine featuring a tang sight, and Orville, with the largest buck and a Model 1873 Winchester. The family that hunts together reaps endless rewards. Photo circa 1925.

BUCKSHOT BRINGS HOME THE BACON
This refined gentleman may be a bit too old to serve his country during the war, but he's not too old to waylay a heavy-bodied 10-pointer with his double-barreled 12 gauge shotgun. Photo circa early 1940s.

COLT'S PATENT FIRE ARMS MANUFACTORY,
HARTFORD, CONN.

HISTORIC COLT FIREARMS FACTORY

Rebuilt in 1867 after a disastrous fire destroyed the building in 1864, the famous Colt Armory (or Colt's Armory) in Hartford, Connecticut was visited by legendary humorist Mark Twain in 1868 who was quite impressed with what he saw.

"It comprises a great range of tall brick buildings," Twain noted, "and on every floor is a dense wilderness of strange iron machines . . . a tangled forest of rods, bars, pulleys, wheels, and all the imaginable and unimaginable forms of mechanism . . . It must have required more brains to invent all those things than would serve to stock 50 Senates like ours."

Today, the site is listed on the National Register of Historic Places in Connecticut and state officials are working with the National Park Service to have it protected and preserved.

SOMEWHERE IN TIME IN THE UPPER MIDWEST

The roof of the log cabin holds a dusting of snow and the hunters have gathered in front of the meat pole with their Marlins and Winchesters and Colt Lightning carbine (third man from right), to capture the moment. Several bragging size bucks hang on the pole. Soon it will be time to divvy up the meat, pack gear and head home. Another magical season will be etched in glorious memory.

This scene has been repeated many times in many different places across this great land for well over a century. Once a year these men gladly leave the comforts of home to spend a week or more in a crowded cabin to share in a special tradition. In addition to the spoils of the hunt, these brave souls will take home a treasure-trove of special memories—the laughs, the pranks, the missed shots, the sharing of deer camp grub, the knowledge that they were able to endure exposure to the weather, the sighting of that first buck standing in the snow on a bone-chilling November morn, seemingly breathing fire as the air escaping from his nostrils turns to vapor. The hunt may be over but the sweet aroma of sizzling bacon, burned toast, tobacco smoke, gun oil, strong coffee and smelly boots will linger in the cabin for many months, and the sounds of bragging voices and snoring on the darkest nights will ring in the rafters forever.

Is it ironic that 13 men are posed with 13 deer? It is sad and difficult to leave camp, to put it all behind for another whole year, but there is a glimmer of hope and one indisputable fact... There is always next year! Photo circa 1910.

The Colt Lightning Carbine or Colt Lightning Rifle was a slide-action rifle manufactured by Colt from 1884 to 1904. It was originally chambered in .44-40. Colt eventually made the Lightning Rifle in three different frame sizes to accommodate a wide range of cartridges, from .22 short and .38-40 to .50-95 Express. It was designed to compete with the pump action and lever-action rifles made by Remington and Winchester. Although it was never as popular as some of the other sporting rifles made in the later 1800s, the Lightning Carbine was always a standout in any deer camp.

"Nevertheless, it is by still-hunting that most deer are killed, and the highest form of hunting craft is shown in the science of the skillful still-hunter. With sufficient practice, any man who possesses common sense, and is both hardy and persevering, can become, to a certain extent, a still-hunter. But the really good still-hunter is born rather than made; though, of course, in addition to possessing the gifts naturally, he must also have developed them, by constant practice, to the highest point possible."

Theodore Roosevelt
Hunting Trips of a Ranchman (1885)

PLEASING THE LITTLE LADY
 The smile on his wife's face says it all. This beaming hunter should be floating on clouds for several reasons. Not only has he managed to waylay a fine spike buck with what appears to be an L.C. Smith-Hunter Arms double gun, but he has also made the "little lady" very happy. Even the dog seems pleased! Photo circa 1925.

CHAPTER 5

DEER TRACKS MAKE MIGHTY THIN SOUP

The first deer hunters in America were rugged pioneers who hunted for food and clothing out of necessity. Later, when the deerhide trade became a prime source of revenue, they began to hunt for profit. Later still, as settlers moved in a westward direction and built communities and towns on the edge of the frontier, they began to hunt because of the tremendous satisfaction it gave them. Deep in their being lived a primordial and primitive man who at one time had to hunt to survive. Deer were plentiful in most areas from the East Coast to the Rocky Mountains. Although most men no longer had to hunt to survive, even those who lived in the cities yearned to get away to the wilderness and hunt for deer.

Long before there were organized sports, hunting for whitetails became a national, all-American pastime. It was never about the killing of an animal. Hunting represented a kind of pureness and freedom found only in the wild places of America. It was a call to adventure that most men craved in one way or another. Being a hunter made a man feel like a real man. Some women also participated with their men and proved to be very adept at shooting and collecting deer.

To many men and women alike, whitetail hunting represented the supreme challenge against a game animal that often was elusive and difficult to hunt. The dangers and hardships that were sometimes involved, both real and perceived, only added to the thrill and excitement of being on one's own and matching wits with a magnificent game animal. Of course men hunted for meat. Taking home a supply of delicious venison was important for a number of reasons, but it was also the icing on the cake.

Marksmanship, reading and interpreting sign, and managing to get along reasonably well in a remote cabin or tent in the hinterlands for a week or longer like their pioneer fathers had done before them was also part of the allure. Facing the elements and roughing it were always challenging. It required strength, endurance and plenty of woods savvy. A man had to have good instincts in the woods. The life of a successful deer hunter required stamina, mastery of certain outdoor skills, patience and plenty of faith. The eternal quest required a rock solid mindset – never give up.

"What'd ya' see out there today, Eddie?"

"I seen some good tracks in the snow."

"Deer tracks make mighty thin soup, Eddie. It's what's in them tracks that'll fill up an empty bowl and a belly."

"Yeah, maybe tomorrow will be different, Seth. Maybe tomorrow will be the day I've been waitin' for all season . . ."

LEAVING WHITETAIL HEAVEN

These men are obviously coming back from a patch of whitetail heaven where they have all succeeded in filling their tags. The photo is a little fuzzy but it certainly tells a story. The man leading the troops and holding the Model '94 Winchester could use some help with his load, but he seems determined to try it on his own for the moment. Photo circa 1915.

FARM COUNTRY BUCK

This hard-working farmhand may look a little rough around the edges, but he knows how to use a shotgun. The back of the photo is dated November 26, 1943 with the inscription: "200-pound deer shot by Hoy!"

"SKINNING THE DEER, NOW A MOOSE BEFORE NIGHTFALL."

The hunter on the right is wearing calf-high Maine Hunting Shoes and holds a Model 94 Winchester. The rifle held by the man sitting appears to be a Marlin 1892 lever-action. Stereoview by American Photo Company, Ilion, New York. Photo probably taken in the Adirondacks, circa early 1900s.

RUMBLE IN THE WOODS
Two well-dressed hunters show off an outstanding eight-point buck in the rumble seat of a 1929 Hupmobile.

NOW THE REAL WORK BEGINS
Deer seem to be hanging everywhere around this rather primitive cabin as one of the hunters takes a knife to the doe in the doorway. The hunter on the right with the stogie in his mouth is holding a Savage 99, while the boy sitting in front of the cabin holds a lever-action rifle. Their camp may be a little sloppy, but these hunters brought home the bacon. Photo circa 1908.

DEER TRACKS MAKE MIGHTY THIN SOUP

"A SUCCESSFUL HUNT"
This determined hunter may be operating on pure adrenaline as he manhandles a fine 8-point buck while his partner carries both rifles. Stereoview by the Whiting Brothers View Co., 1903.

TWO LUCKY GUYS
These hunters couldn't be more thrilled if they'd bagged a new world record whitetail. Dated November 15, 1954, the back of the photo is inscribed: "Red and Joe – lucky guys."

BACK HOME WITH THEIR BOUNTY

The six bucks taken by these dedicated Pennsylvania deer slayers have drawn a crowd in front of Steve Nichols Buick-Pontiac dealership in Hamburg, Pennsylvania. For many years the dealership was a well-known business in Hamburg. Note the young man on the left displaying his pistol. Photo circa 1930.

WHAT A REAL BUCK LOOKS LIKE!

Posed with his long-barreled Marlin 1894 lever-action rifle, a proud Mr. Partee had one whale of a day in the deer woods. Addressed to Marjorie Foster, the back of this picture postcard reads: "Dear Margie, Uncle Simon sends you this. It is Mr. Partee and the deer he shot. Simon says show it to Uncle John so he will know how they look. Maybe he can get one next time he goes hunting." No indication is given as to the location, but it likely comes from the Upper Midwest, circa 1910.

DEER TRACKS MAKE MIGHTY THIN SOUP

"DEER HUNTING"

Postcard dated December 1911, addressed to Howes Corners, Maine, with the following inscription: "Wish you was here. Have not got anything yet but have not been out but one day yet." Signed, "A.E.G."

A RIP-ROARING DAY

With no visible horns showing, it looks like these proud young men have done a good day's work with three fine does on the meat pole. The hunter on the left is holding a small-caliber bolt-action rifle (could it be a .22 for small game?), while the two hunters on the right are each wielding single-barrel shotguns. The gun on the far right appears to be a Stevens. With a little snow on the ground and some obviously cool temperatures, it's been another rip-roaring day in the deer woods. Photo circa 1925.

SHIRTTAILS COME CHEAP

The ritual of losing one's shirttail after missing a deer is an American tradition that goes way back. Here, a smiling Ranger Arthur Woody looks on as his good friend Charlie Elliott goes through the ordeal of losing his shirttail after missing a shot at a buck during a historic 1940 firearms deer hunt in the mountains of North Georgia. At the time this photo was taken, Elliott was Commissioner of Georgia Natural Resources Department. Elliott loses yet another shirttail in a November 1949 story he penned for *Outdoors* magazine. It seems he was a glutton for punishment, but in truth, he was just being a good sport. Both photos were no doubt staged for the camera.

Elliott enjoyed an extensive career in conservation and wildlife management during the 1930s and '40s. In 1950, he became southeastern field editor for *Outdoor Life*, a position he held for 40 years. He wrote hundreds of articles about big game hunting across North America and some 20 books during his long and productive career.

In 1946, popular American cartoonist Ed Dodd used the pipe-smoking Charlie Elliott as his model for Mark Trail, a comic strip character whose mission as a conservation officer was to preserve wildlife, wild places and water resources for future generations. The syndicated comic strip, now dealing more with environmental issues, still runs in about 175 newspapers worldwide.

Known to many simply as "Mr. Chollie," and in turkey-hunting circles as "the Old Professor," Charlie Elliott died in 2000 at the age of 94.

Long time outdoor sports writer Charlie Elliott.

DEER TRACKS MAKE MIGHTY THIN SOUP **75**

TO CARRY A DEER
"Something's not right. Is this the way you do it?"

"Ah, much better. I'll get the hang of this deer toting sooner or later."

HEADING TO CAMP
"Two old men, two old guns on a long walk back through time."
— Old Hunter's Quote

"This is so much easier . . . Why didn't I think of this to start with?" At 5,267-feet, Mt. Katahdin in Maine looms on the horizon. Photos circa 1920s, northern Maine.

A COLD DAY IN NORTHERN MICHIGAN
These rugged hunters in northern Michigan are preparing to leave the warmth of their tent and face the elements. Although conditions may be brutal, they know a day like this is the perfect time to shoot a good buck. Photo circa 1910.

THE WEARY HUNTERS AMID NEW ENGLAND'S SNOWY HILLS
The outside temperature may be brutal, but this successful quartet is not feeling the cold. Their hearts have been warmed by the heavy exertions of the day and the results of their hunt. Stereoview by B.W. Kilburn, Littleton, New Hampshire, circa 1900.

A DAILY DOUBLE?
The moon of the rutting stag apparently cast its spell on this hefty ridge-runner and turned out to be his undoing. Was he chasing the doe when the lucky hunter caught up with him? If so, some quick thinking and rifle action must have occurred because it's not easy bringing down a buck and doe at the same time. This is one farm family that will be eating well come winter. Photo circa 1910.

FOLK TALES FROM THE SOUTHERN APPALACHIANS

No whitetail hunting history would be complete without a few classic folk tales that date back to some of the first American hunters around Daniel Boone's time. The theme of making every shot count is as old as the southern highlands that spawned it. In the old days, powder and ball were expensive commodities. Many variations of the following two stories have been told.

"The Jackpot Shot" is built around the central theme of a young hunter sent out to fetch supper by his father and given one ball with which to accomplish the task. Many an old southern hunter who grew up during or after the Great Depression of the 1930s can well relate to that experience.

"A Great Hunter" is built around the theme of adapting to conditions in order to "make meat."

Note: Both photos showcase flintlock rifles made by Jack Crockford in the 1950s and '60s. The first is a rifle, possibles bag, powder horn and priming horn. The second shows Jack Crockford aiming one of his finely-crafted flintlock rifles. See Chapter 15 for more on Crockford. The second photo was taken by iconic *Atlanta Constitution* photographer Kenneth Rogers, circa 1960.

THE JACKPOT SHOT

An old-timer went huntin' alongside a big stream with his muzzleloader. He had plenty of powder in his powder horn, but only enough lead shot in his pouch to make one more shot. He looked up and saw a turkey perched on the limb of a tree that stood on the bank of a stream. So he loaded his rifle with what he knew would be his last load, and he prepared to shoot the turkey. Just then, he saw a deer standing under the tree that the turkey was in. At the same time he heard a buzzing sound near the bank of the stream. He looked down. Coiled on the ground a few feet away lay a nervous rattlesnake. The old hunter decided to take his chances and shoot the turkey anyway. He aimed and fired. Being a little nervous because of the snake, his shot pattern went a little low. Part of his load hit the turkey, killing him dead; the other part hit the limb the turkey was on. The limb fell on the deer below, killing him dead. The ramrod fell out of the old hunter's rifle, killing the snake dead. Upon firing the gun, the recoil kicked the old hunter back into the deep water of the stream. When he came up, his shirttail was filled with fish.

The happy hunter carried home a deer, a turkey and several fish, not to mention the rattlesnake, all the result of one last load of shot!

A GREAT HUNTER

An old preacher, who was also known to be a great hunter, loved to spin the following yarn:

"I once went to Round Hill a-huntin'. Now the base of the hill forms a perfect circle with a thick forest around it. When I neared the hill, a buck started up and took out around it. I followed for some time, but could not get a shot. So I bent my gun barrel across my knee to correspond with the curve of the hill and fired. The bullet followed the buck and killed him dead. I went on to where the buck had fallen and straightened the barrel. Near at hand, I saw some honey running out of a tree, where the ball had entered after passing through the buck. I drove a peg in the tree to hold in the honey until I could return. I cut off the hindquarters of the buck, slung 'em across my shoulder and headed home. I had on a very large and loose pair of pants which turned out to my advantage, for when I reached the creek, the water was up and I had to wade across. When I got to the other side of the creek, I took fifteen pounds of jumping perch out of my pants. A few days later, me and my friends went back and got five pounds of splendid honey out of that tree. You may easily understand how we lived on deer, honey and fish for some time."

THE ARTFUL WHITETAIL
Special full color section

PREVIOUS PAGE:

A CHRISTMAS DEER

Acclaimed magazine illustrator Lynn Bogue Hunt painted *A Christmas Deer* for the December 1947 cover of *Field & Stream*. It's an oil on canvas.

A GOOD CHANCE

Early American hunters sometimes drove deer to water with dogs where they could be easily dispatched. Hunters also liked to paddle quietly in backwater areas where they could slip up on feeding deer. Painted by Arthur F. Tait. Lithograph by Currier & Ives, 1863.

ON THE RUN

On the Run is among many images of North American big game created by Tom Beecham (1926-2000). In the early 1950s Beecham was a successful commercial Illustrator in New York. He began painting around 1973, after years of illustrating scantily clad women, cowboys fighting Native Americans, and jungle scenes with Amazonian natives. *On the Run* is from the collection of Remington Arms, which used the image on one of their popular calendars.

THE ARTFUL WHITETAIL

"FIRST SNOW – 1855"
Hunters sneaking up on winter deer yard. Painted by Arthur F. Tait. Lithograph by Nathaniel Currier, 1855.

"AMERICAN WINTER SPORTS – DEER SHOOTING ON THE SHATTAGEE"
Two backwoods hunters are stalking deer along backwaters of the Shattagee River. "Shattagee" may be an old nickname for a real tributary or river in Pennsylvania or New York. Painting by L. Maurer. Lithograph by Nathaniel Currier, 1855.

THE HANSON BUCK

Acclaimed wildlife artist Ron Van Gilder painted The Hanson Buck, the reigning number one typical whitetail in the Boone & Crockett record books. Van Gilder visited Milo Hanson at his Saskatchewan farm and was granted permission to create this first-ever painting of the monster buck. Hanson was carrying his Winchester Model 88 lever-action .308 on the morning of November 23, 1993, when he shot the huge 12-pointer, which scored 213 5/8 inches.

"A MAINE HUNTING SCENE"

Although the title denotes Maine, two large mule deer bucks lay in the snow with at least one large whitetail buck, and a whitetail skin hangs from the tree. This photo was probably taken in Montana, not Maine. Color postcard circa 1911.

THE ARTFUL WHITETAIL

"THE LIFE OF A HUNTER – CATCHING A TARTAR."
The life of a hunter can sometimes be filled with danger and unexpected consequences. Painting by Arthur F. Tait. Lithograph by Currier & Ives, 1861.

"B&A SERIES, ON THE MOOSE RIVER."
Two men paddling up a backwater of the Moose River in northern Maine with a nice buck in the canoe. Color Postcard, 1907.

"DEER DRIVING, 1857"

Arthur F. Tait painted several versions of this scene. This one depicts not only the two hunters in a canoe, a swimming dog and a buck on shore running into the woods, but it also includes the added element of a swimming buck that has been caught and apparently subdued by one of the hunters alongside the canoe. Doesn't that man know he's got a handful of dynamite? Lithograph by Nathaniel Currier, 1857.

OLD THREE LEGS

Old Three Legs by popular Minnesota wildlife artist Les Kouba (1917-1998) now hangs in the McLeod County Historical Society. Image courtesy of Leskoubaoutdoors.com. (See page 192).

THE ARTFUL WHITETAIL 87

SURPRISE!
 Bob Kuhn was a masterful storyteller with his brush and acrylic paints. Here, two hunters carrying out their doe are surprised by a buck well within range of their rifles. They'll never forget this unexpected encounter. Courtesy Remington Arms.

"RESULT OF A FAIR DAY'S HUNT, HIGHLANDS OF ONTARIO."
These satisfied hunters have had more than a "fair" day. Looks like every man got what he came for. Color Postcard, circa 1907.

"WAITING FOR THE FREIGHT"
Two young moose bulls and a lone whitetail doe await the train that will transport them back to civilization along with the happy group of hunters who bagged them. In addition to several Winchester rifles, the man in the white sweater at left holds a C96 Mauser pistol with a rifle stock. Color postcard circa 1920.

THE ARTFUL WHITETAIL

BUCKS ONLY
Bob Kuhn (1920-2007) is widely hailed as the greatest painter of wild animals—ever. After graduating from prestigious Pratt Institute in Brooklyn New York, he would become one of the most popular wildlife illustrators in America before turning to easel painting full time in 1970. Kuhn traveled around the world to obtain inspiration for his paintings of wildlife. *Bucks Only* is reproduced courtesy of Remington Arms.

WIDE OPEN
Bob Kuhn's drawing skills were unmatched in the world of wildlife art. In fact, almost every one of his acrylic paintings began with a pencil or pen-and-ink drawing such as this sketch of a bounding whitetail.

"GOOD DEER HUNTING IN THE LOWER RIO GRANDE VALLEY OF TEXAS."
Color Postcard circa 1911.

DEADFALL
Connecticut sporting artist Chet Reneson has painted hunting and fishing scenes from Maine to the Caribbean. In this intriguing watercolor, a hunter approaches his buck that expired just as it was trying to leap a massive deadfall.

THE ARTFUL WHITETAIL **91**

"TWO STAMFORD SPORTS, STAMFORD, NEW YORK"
The sport on the left is holding a Winchester lever-action while the older gentleman on the right appears to be holding a single-shot shotgun. Photo circa 1909.

RUBBING TIME
Tom Beecham painted this whitetail busily polishing his antlers on a small sapling. The image appeared on one of Remington's popular calendars.

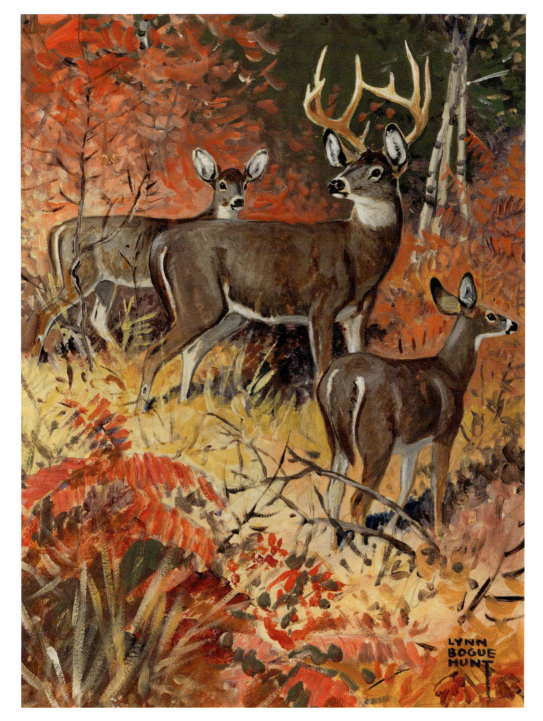

WHITETAIL FAMILY
Lynn Bogue Hunt painted this watercolor on board in the 1940s.

FOLLOWING PAGES:

THREE GENERATIONS
When acclaimed artist John Banovich first saw these monster bucks at a friend's farm north of Manhattan, New York, he knew he had to paint them. "To say they inspired me would be an understatement," said Banovich. "These massive bucks ran with such lithe grace that it would have been a crime to paint them any other way."

THE ARTFUL WHITETAIL

END OF THE DAY
 Talented sporting artist Brett Smith enjoys painting hunters and fishermen in colorful scenes from yesteryear. Here, two hunters in 1930s' apparel close out a successful day of hunting deer and waterfowl.

Chapter 6

MR. BROWNING MADE A GUN:
JOHN MOSES BROWNING (1855-1926)

John Browning had a gift for understanding mechanics and an amazing vision for making revolutionary gun designs. He was a genius. The debt American hunters, riflemen and soldiers owe this man is enormous. He came from a Morman family of 22 children. His father, Jonathan Browning, was a gifted gunmaker in his own right who had invented a repeating rifle with a revolving cylinder.

With his father's full support and encouragement, young John made his first gun at age 10 in his father's shop. Later, he and four of his brothers followed in their father's footsteps and opened a shop in their hometown of Ogden in 1879, then part of the Utah Territory.

Young John had invented and patented a revolutionary new falling-breech single-shot rifle. The Browning Gun Factory opened its doors with the intention of manufacturing the new rifle. However, Winchester soon bought the rights to the gun and the famous Winchester single-shot rifle established the young gunmaker's reputation as well as his future association with Winchester. Although the rifle had a single trigger guard, it was strikingly similar in appearance to one of Browning's first lever-action rifles that would come along a few years later.

In fact, Winchester quickly acquired the rights to produce Browning's innovative new design for a lever-action rifle, and the world-famous Winchester Model 1886 repeating rifle was born. The models 1892, 1894 and 1895 soon followed the '86, and John Browning was well on his way toward becoming the Thomas Edison of the firearms industry.

During his career, John Browning obtained 128 gun patents that eventually spawned the production of some 80 guns. Some were produced by his own firm, but most were made by Winchester, Remington, Colt, Savage and Fabrique Nationale de Guerre in Belgium.

In addition to the iconic lever-action rifles that Browning perfected, he also patented a lever-action shotgun, a pump-action shotgun, a semi-automatic shotgun, the Remington Model 8 semi-automatic sporting rifle, the M2 .50-caliber machine gun, the Browning Automatic Rifle (BAR), and the classic Colt Model 1911, .45 caliber semi-automatic handgun that saw action in World War I, World War II and the Korean War.

Browning was a lifelong member of The Church of Jesus Christ of Latter-day Saints. He died at his desk of heart failure in 1926 at the age of 71 while working on a new pistol design.

LONE STAR BONANZA

Four turkey gobblers and two nice bucks—these Lone Star hunters have had an extraordinary day's outing with their ever-reliable Remington Model 81 Woodmaster rifles. During the first half of the 20th century, before turkey restoration got underway in a number of eastern states where numbers had reached dangerously low levels, and before "shotgun only" laws were passed in many of those same states, deer hunters in Texas and other states often preferred to hunt gobblers with their favorite deer rifles. These two '81s are prime examples. Photo circa 1941.

"The Winchester, which is stocked and sighted to suit myself, is by all odds the best weapon I ever had, and I now use it almost exclusively, having killed every kind of game with it from a grizzly bear to a bighorn. It is as handy to carry, whether on foot or on horseback, and comes to the shoulder as readily as a shotgun; it is absolutely sure, and there is no recoil to jar and disturb the aim, while it carries accurately quite as far as a man can aim with any degree of certainty. The Winchester is the best gun to be found in the United States, for it is as deadly, accurate, and handy as any, stands very rough usage, and it is unapproachable for the rapidity of fire and the facility with which it is loaded."

Theodore Roosevelt
Hunting Trips of a Ranchman, 1885

BROWNING AND MODEL 11
John M. Browning proudly holds one of his most enduring inventions, the Browning A-5 Humpback automatic shotgun (Remington Model 11). During his remarkable career, Browning obtained 128 different gun patents that eventually saw the successful production of some 80 firearms.

SUCCESS IS CONTAGIOUS
A pair of Savage 99s, a couple of Remington Model 25 pump guns, and a lever-action rifle accounted for at least two fine bucks. These well-outfitted young hunters may be from the city, but they certainly appear to know what they're doing. Furthermore, they're having a grand time doing it! The New York license tag on the early-1920s Buick Roadster is dated 1924. How did they all pile into that small car with their guns and gear?

THE LION MAN
This handsome young hunter must know what he's doing. Armed with a half-magazine Winchester Model 1892, he's made short work of these three big cats. John Browning's Model '92 was a lighter and smaller version of the Model 1886. Interestingly, as one of the "guns that won the West," some 50 or 60 years after this photo was taken, the easy-handling '92 carbine was immortalized by John Wayne in dozens of his classic westerns. It was also the rifle of choice for Chuck Connors in *The Rifleman* TV series, and by Steve McQueen in *Wanted Dead or Alive*. Hollywood notwithstanding, the '92 was an ideal hunting rifle for many species of North American big game. Photo circa 1905.

THE WINCHESTER 1895 STRIKES AGAIN
Still wearing his snowshoes and holding his trusty Winchester 1895, you have to wonder: How long did this determined hunter stay on the track of this mule deer buck before he got close enough for a shot? He also got a young deer. Unlike some of the early Winchesters, the '95 was the first lever-action rifle with a magazine to accept the smokeless "hi-powered" rounds that soon revolutionized the hunting world. Photo circa 1910.

Designed by John Browning, the 1895 Winchester was the first non-detachable box magazine rifle that Winchester produced. It was chambered for such high-power smokeless cartridges as .30-40 Krag, .38-72 Winchester, .40-72 Winchester, .303 British, .35 Winchester, .405 Government, 7.62 Russian, .30-03, and .30-06. Former President Theodore Roosevelt and his son, Kermit, took along three Model '95s on their classic African trip in 1909; two in .405 Government and one in .30-03.

EARLY SEASON BOUNTY

With the day's bounty tied over his shoulder, this young hunter is making easy work of getting his deer out of the woods. Hunting on the Garner Ranch in the San Jacinto Mountains of southern California in August 1914, he has just bagged a young, early-season blacktail buck. The velvet buck was taken with his ever-dependable Winchester '94 carbine.

The original '94 was chambered to fire the .32-40 Winchester and the .38-55 Winchester, both being metallic, black powder cartridges. A year later the '94 became the first repeating rifle in America to use smokeless powder, being chambered to fire the .30 WCF or .30-30 cartridge. Other calibers were soon offered, including the .25-35 Winchester and the loved-by-some .32 Winchester Special. Designed through the amazing engineering genius of John Browning in 1894, the Model 94 was destined to become one of the most popular deer hunting rifles of all time. Photo circa 1914.

JOHN AND HIS BUCK

According to this photo postcard, a proud young man named John shot this spike buck in November of 1915. John's half-magazine Winchester '92 lever action has a 24-inch octagon barrel. Wonder if the rifle belongs to his dad.

HOW THEY LOVE THEIR WINCHESTER RIFLES

From left, in the photo above: This hunter appears to have a shorter barreled '73 carbine. The popular Model 1873 came in .32-20, .38-40 and .44-40 calibers and could be purchased with 24- or 26-inch barrels. Barrels were round, octagon or half-octagon. The man smoking a pipe is holding a Winchester Model 10 semi-automatic. Very similar to the Model 1907, the '10 was chambered in .401 caliber. The middle man also has a lever-action '73. The fourth hunter is holding a Model 1873 with a half magazine. The last man is aiming his Winchester Model 1873, long-barreled repeater. This photo was taken somewhere in the Adirondacks, circa 1915.

WHAT A TROPHY!

Two proud hunters show off the head of a fine 10-point buck. The rifle responsible for the deed is a popular Winchester Model 1892 takedown with a 24-inch round barrel. The original '92 was available in .38-40, .32-20 and .44-40 centerfire. Later models offered several more calibers.

Admiral Robert E. Peary carried a '92 to the North Pole in 1892 and famed hunter Sasha Siemel, known for hunting South American jaguars with a spear, used a short-barreled '92 carbine with an attached bayonet as backup on several of his daring jungle hunts. Photo circa 1900.

HAPPY HUNTER

A beaming Robert Allen proudly shows off his first buck, taken with a Model 94 Winchester carbine. Photo circa early 1950s.

VINTAGE CABINET PHOTOS

Since these photos were produced in a studio in Chehalis, Washington in the early 1900s, the buck pictured in this collection may well be a Columbian whitetail. The western-most deer of any whitetail subspecies, Columbian whitetails were first seen by Lewis and Clark in 1805. They were nearly wiped out in the early 1900s as a result of over-hunting. Listed as an endangered species in 1965, they were removed from that list in 2005 and once again can be hunted in limited numbers in some areas of the state. Photo circa early 1900s.

Two hunters with Winchester lever-action carbines tote their young buck to camp. The man on the left holds a Winchester '94, saddle ring carbine, while his companion wields a Winchester '92.

These hunters crossing a large stream with their dog and their bounty are identified in the cabinet photo as Frank Hoch on the left and Anton Taylor on the right. Their rifles appear to be Winchester '92s.

After an exhilarating day in the woods, it's time to take off the boots, rest the feet and sit in the shade. An assortment of lever guns, a good dog and some fine vittles in the making creates a memorable scene.

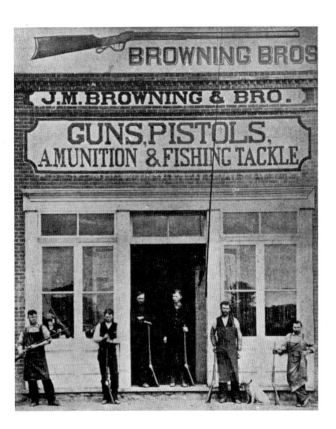

THE BROWNING BOYS
The first Shop and Arms Factory. John and Matt Browning are shown in the doorway. Left to right are Sam, George, John, Matt and Ed Browning and an unidentified gunsmith. Right: Winchester "Bag a Buck" ad for Model 94, Model 70 and Model 12 shotgun, 1949.

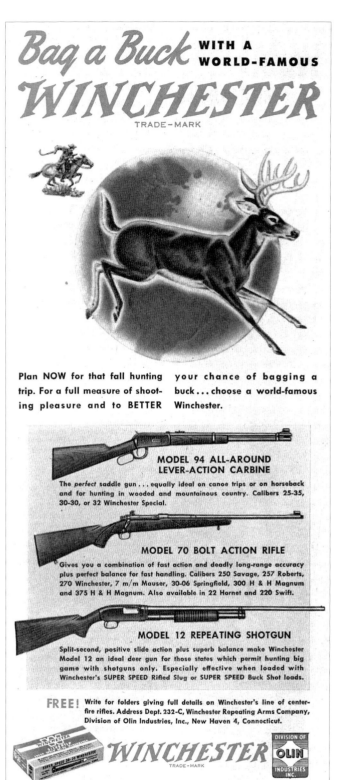

THE TIMELESS WINCHESTER MODEL 1892
Winchester Repeating Arms Company produced upwards of one million Model 1892 rifles from 1892 to 1938 out of their New Haven, Connecticut location. Carbine forms of the rifle remained in production well into the early 1940s. The Model 1892 was chambered for the .32-20, .38-40 and .44-40 cartridges. The popular .25-20 became available in 1895 and the .218 Bee cartridge in 1936.

BUCKSHOT AND VENISON

Written on the front of this weathered photo are the words: "One of Billie's Bucks, Black Hawk Lake, 1911." Billie is holding a Stevens 520 pump shotgun, probably a 12 gauge. The Stevens Model 520, and the later 521 and 522 models, were pump-action shotguns developed by John Browning and originally manufactured by the J Stevens Arms & Tool Company between 1909 and 1916. Billie might have hailed from Iowa. Black Hawk Lake, named for Chief Black Hawk, is a 957-acre glacier lake in Sac County, Iowa. Billie might have found some good whitetail hunting there in 1911.

WINCHESTER COUNTRY

For some hunters, it's a matter of being in the right place at the right time. For others, it's dedication and patience. With several fine bucks hanging, these Winchester boys have seemingly made their own luck with their array of trusty Winchester '94 carbines. Photo circa 1898.

AN ARSENAL OF WINCHESTER RIFLES
 These proud hunters will soon be adding to the array of bleached-out whitetail racks hanging on the roof of their log cabin (note the brick chimney). Armed with a small arsenal of newfangled Winchester lever-action rifles and carbines that shoot smokeless powder, this group seems to be taking two things quite seriously: hunting and eating. After all, how many Midwestern hunting clubs in the late 19th century were able to enjoy the culinary delights of a camp cook? No doubt, there'll be some mouthwatering rabbit stew and venison roast awaiting this bunch when they return from the afternoon hunt. For now, it's time to put the camera aside, unchain the hound and go rouse up a nice buck or two. Photo circa 1900.

MR. BROWNING MADE A GUN

WINCHESTER MODEL 94
John Browning's Model 1894 lever-action rifle manufactured by Winchester was the first commercial repeating rifle built to be used with smokeless powder. It was originally chambered for the .32-40 Winchester and .38-55 Winchester metallic black powder cartridges. Winchester Arms went to a different steel composition in 1895 that could handle higher pressure rounds and offered the Model 94 in .25-35 Winchester and .30-30 Winchester. In 1899, the Model '94 was also chambered in .32 Winchester Special, but the faithful .30-30 became the darling of the lever-action repeaters and the Model 94 Winchester became the most legendary deer rifle of all time.

BUCK IN A SIDECAR
Normally, this handsome young man might have his pretty girlfriend sitting next to him in the sidecar, but today is different. His long-barreled Winchester Model 1894, probably manufactured in the early 1900s, bears witness to the fact that he's been pursuing a different type of "dear," and his efforts were not in vain. Since two rifles are pictured, a hunting companion was likely with him on this memorable adventure. Photo circa 1924.

PRIDE OF THE ADIRONDACKS
Opening Day of the 1946 season found avid New York hunter Bill Mundell sneaking through the woods with his guide near Big Moose Lake in the heart of the Adirondack Mountains. This fine young buck fell to his ever-reliable Remington Model 81.

THE ENDURING MODELS 8 AND 81

The Remington Model 8 was a highly popular semi-automatic rifle designed by John Browning and produced by Remington. The Model 8 was the first commercially successful semi-automatic rifle offered to sportsmen in the United States. It was introduced as the Remington Autoloading Rifle in 1905, but the name was changed to the Remington Model 8 in 1911. Remington offered the rifle in four calibers: .25 Remington, .30 Remington, .32 Remington and .35 Remington. The rifle was an immediate hit among deer hunters. Remington produced the popular Model 8 until 1936, at which time it was replaced by the similar but upgraded Model 81 Woodmaster.

Interestingly, the Model 8 was the gun of choice for Texas Ranger Frank Hamer, the famous lawman who caught up with Bonnie Parker and Clyde Barrow and ended their long crime spree on May 23, 1934 in Gibsland, Louisiana. Hamer's personal rifle was a custom .35 Remington with a special-ordered 15-round magazine that he purchased from Petmeckey's Sporting Goods Store in Austin, Texas. (See page 174 in Volume 1 of *Dawn of American Deer Hunting* for a photo of the famous store). Reportedly at least two Model 8s were used during the ambush of Bonnie and Clyde.

THE VERSATILE '92

Standing in a grove of birch trees, these all-American young men are obviously proud of their day's bounty, a fine buck and doe, taken with their ever-dependable Winchesters. Have they found deer-hunting heaven with their Winchester '92s? If not, it's gotta be close. Circa late 1890s, early 1900s.

PANHANDLE POSSE
The photos seem to tell us the young hunter on the left is posing with the buck he just brought down. He was using a Winchester Model 1905 or 1907 self-loader shown in the photo above. The older gentleman on the right probably was using the Remington Model 11 shotgun. The photos likely come from Texas or Oklahoma, circa 1925.

THE BROWNING A-5 "HUMPBACK" (REMINGTON MODEL 11)
The Browning Auto-5 was designed by John Browning in 1898 and patented in 1900. Winchester turned him down as a potential manufacturer so he contracted with a company in Europe for production. The first A-5s were made in Belgium in 1902. Remington licensed the design as its Model 11 and the gun sold well from 1905 to 1947. Later, Savage Arms successfully sold Browning's design as the Model 720 from 1930 to 1949. The A-5 remained in production until 1998, seeing almost a full century of service and becoming legendary in the process. It was the first mass-produced semi-automatic shotgun in America.

WHITETAIL COUNTRY
Labeled "Thornapple, Nov. 1900," this hunting cabin might have been in Thornapple Township just south of Grand Rapids, Michigan. The Thornapple River runs nearby. The area has long been good whitetail country. These two gents appear to be seasoned hunters. The man on the left is wielding a slide-action 12-gauge Winchester Model '97, a popular shotgun that sold well in the early 20th century. Of course, it was designed and perfected by none other than John Moses Browning.

Browning introduced the first repeating shotgun, a lever-action model, in 1887, but it was considered somewhat awkward to use. In 1893 he introduced his first pump model shotgun. By 1897, he had eliminated most of the flaws, and the '97 sold well for the next 60 years. Chambered in 12 and 16 gauge, the basic Model 97 sold for $25 around 1900. The man on the right is holding something with a large bore, but it's hard to say what.

MR. BROWNING MADE A GUN **111**

"Twice have I seen a big buck drive the does and smaller deer out of their covert to be hunted, while he himself lay down in their hiding place and let the chase go by. For the hunters, of course, seeing a deer jump and run, never dreaming of looking in the thicket out of which the buck had driven them and in which he lay watching the effect cunningly."

Following the Deer,
William J. Long, 1903

SOLO HUNTER
This 9-point heavyweight was taken in Vermont's Windsor County in the early 1900s. Although we know the young hunter was using a Winchester Model 94 rifle, his name is unknown.

CHAPTER 7

THE BUCK STOPS HERE:
VERMONT'S AMAZING WHITETAIL HERITAGE

Deer, bear, moose and other wildlife species disappeared at an alarming rate in Vermont as the 19th century progressed. Since timber was one of the state's most valuable cash crops and economic resources, old growth forests were clear-cut with no thought of regeneration or managing future forests as renewable resources. The prevailing philosophy seemed to be "cut every tree on the mountain and when they're all gone, move to another location and repeat the process." Forests in America were endless, and little thought was given to the damage inflicted on the land.

By the middle part of the century, big game populations had reached dangerously low numbers across the state. In 1865, deer hunting in Vermont was outlawed. No legal hunting for deer occurred for the next 32 years. During this time, the few deer that remained were well protected. Some deer were brought in from New York and restocked in areas containing the fewest animals.

While this was happening, an unforeseen event took place in the late 1800s that benefited the growing deer herd immensely. Scores of played-out farms that had been cleared of forests and undergrowth since colonial days were abandoned. Thousands of acres reverted back to nature and became prime deer habitat at a time when the newly restored herd needed it the most.

By 1898, deer numbers had increased to such sustainable levels that a limited season was opened in October of that year. In all, 103 bucks fell to delighted Vermont hunters. Many of the bucks carried exceptional racks and body weights because they were older animals.

With the vision and leadership of far-sighted individuals like President Theodore Roosevelt, the early 20th century saw the mindset of the country slowly shift from one of exploitation to wise use and conservation of precious resources. The concepts of wildlife and timber management became new sciences.

Deer populations continued to grow in Vermont and elsewhere as management practices were implemented and as habitat continued to improve. Conventional wisdom dictated that "bucks only" could be legally killed by Vermont hunters. Does were as sacred as cows walking the streets of Calcutta, India. This diehard bucks-only policy continued in Vermont and other states for the next 50 years.

During the first half of the 20th century, Vermont's deer herd continued to grow. In 1940, hunters legally bagged 4,000 bucks. By the time World War II ended, biologists were beginning to see signs of over-browsing in some areas where deer numbers were beginning to exceed the carrying capacity of the land. Deer managers realized the only way to control total numbers was through the legal shooting of does. But the majority of Vermont hunters wanted no part of killing does and the issue was hotly debated. It took decades before hunters finally condoned the shooting of does as a vital management tool.

While most hunters were more interested in body weights than antler sizes in the early 1900s, many outstanding bucks were taken in Vermont. This trend continued right up into the 1950s.

The following photos represent a small sample of some of the true Green Mountain State "slobberknockers" that hunters brought home during those unforgettable good ol' days!

Special thanks to Curtis Smiley of the Vermont Big Game Trophy Club for graciously providing these photographs.

BUCK HORN CAMP
Some fine bucks hang on the meat pole at Buck Horn Camp in 1911. By the early 1900s, much abandoned farmland in Vermont had gone back to nature, creating ideal deer habitat for the expanding herd.

A BRUTE OF A DEER
Delbert Locke was hunting in Lamoille County with a Winchester Model 94 half magazine when he encountered this eight-point brute. Photo circa, 1913.

Newspaper clipping of Frank Goodenough.

VERMONT DOUBLE
Frank Goodenough of West Bridgewater poses with two fine bucks taken in Windsor County. Apparently it was legal to shoot two bucks per season in those days. Frank was using his trusty ol' Winchester '73. No doubt that rifle accounted for plenty of game over the years. Photo circa 1910.

SHOWCASE BUCK
Hunter John Drew shot this impressive 10-pointer in Addison County in 1953.

THE MODEL 16 STRIKES AGAIN
John Irwin poses with a fine Essex County buck taken during the 1940s. His rifle appears to be a short-lived Remington Model 16 semiautomatic, introduced in 1916. The Model 16 was chambered for a brand-new bullet, the .22 Remington Automatic, a rimfire round developed in 1915 exclusively for that gun. The bullets were loaded into the back of the stock. The Model 16 fired a 45-grain bullet that traveled approximately 950 feet per second, with 90 foot-pounds of muzzle energy. Because of the slightly larger diameter of the case, the cartridge was not interchangeable with .22 short, long or long rifle guns.

The Model 16 seems under-gunned for a 250-pound Vermont buck, but some hunters back in the day used very light calibers with continual success. Remington discontinued the Model 16 in 1928 because the bullet never really caught on.

A BEEF OR A BUCK?
An elated Robert Perkins admires the massive buck he shot in Orange County in 1949. This huge-bodied beast has a 10-point rack to match his weight.

ONE FOR THE WALL
This gnarly non-typical was taken by Bertie Hilliard in Burlington County in 1937.

COOL AND COLLECTED
A confident LeRoy Marsha leans against a late 1930s Ford coup holding the outstanding buck he shot in Orange County sometime during the early 1940s. LeRoy is sporting a Winchester Model 1894 carbine. A second carbine rests against the car.

RENOWNED DEER HUNTER
Nationally acclaimed whitetail hunter Larry Benoit of Duxbury poses with several 200-plus-pound bucks taken in Vermont and adjoining states, circa early 1970s. For much more on Larry, see Chapter 15.

"OLD GOLDEN"
Leo Brown was perhaps 17 or 18 when he downed this multi-tined buck during the November season near East Richford in Franklin County. The buck reportedly dressed out at 327 pounds.
According to Leo's son, Elmer, in a story appearing in the *Vermont Sportsman* decades later, "Old Golden, the name given this deer by many hunters who had tried in vain to bag him, fell one evening at dusk after Dad had waited for him in an abandoned house. Old Golden was so tough he could hardly be eaten." Photo circa 1915.

LOVE THAT MARLIN
Loyerston Bovey managed to outwit this picture-perfect 8-pointer in Bennington County during the 1925 season. Bovey accomplished his feat using a Marlin Model 1893 lever-action. The lightweight, easy-handling rifle, featuring a half magazine with a round, 24-inch standard barrel, was a popular choice among New England hunters in the 1920s.

This particular rifle, boasting Marlin's ingenious side ejection feature, was probably manufactured in the early 1900s. Over time, the '93 was chambered in .25-36, .30-30, .32 Special, .32-40 and .38-55. In 1936 the rifle was renamed the Model 1936. It was later shortened to the Model 36, which stayed in production until 1948.

A BONA FIDE VERMONT TROPHY
New Hampshire hunter Perley Whipple shot this extraordinary wallhanger in Essex County, Vermont, in 1960. The man standing next to him holding the Model 94 Winchester may be Perley's father.

TWO BUCKS ON A BUICK

A smiling Reginald Sanders and his hunting partner Harold Kimball struck paydirt in Orange County, Vermont during the '51 season. Reginald used a bolt-action rifle to down his beautiful nine-pointer, while Harold's spike buck fell to a scoped Savage Model 99 (probably a Model 99RSII, produced after World War II).

A MAGICAL HUNT

The 1951 season proved to be a magical time for avid deer hunter Ralph Ray. Using his smooth-shooting Marlin Model 1893 lever-action, Ralph shot this 10-point bruiser in Washington County.

A SPECIAL ADMIRER
This hefty spike buck fell to a Winchester Model 94 .30-30 carbine in Bennington County, Vermont in 1907. Sadly, the young hunter's name as well as that of his young brother or son are lost to the ages.

> "To put an old lean-flanked, rough-shod veteran (like a trophy whitetail) on the spot, you have to be smarter than he is; and outguessing a buck is a feat in mental gymnastics."
>
> Archibald Rutledge
> *Those Were the Days* (1955)

THE COLDER, THE BETTER
It's a frigid day near Hannibal, Wisconsin and these seasoned riflemen know they need a stout meat pole to hold this much venison. Most of the rifles appear to be lever-action Winchesters, although the fourth man from left holds either a Model 1907 or 1910 Winchester self-loading semi-automatic. It's hard to say what nationality these hearty individuals represent, but they are definitely an ethnic group so typical of the many immigrants who settled in northern Wisconsin. Photo courtesy of state historical society of Wisconsin, circa 1910.

CHAPTER 8

WELCOME TO THE DEER WOODS:
NOTHING LIKE IT IN THE WORLD

If you ask 100 different hunters to give you a definition of deer camp, you're apt to get 100 different answers. The remote deer camps of yesteryear were a blend of countless personalities and rich traditions. While a simple definition might be "a far-off place where friends and family gather each year during deer season and share experiences and new adventures while deer hunting," it goes so much deeper. In truth, there is nothing like it in the world. And while there are many similarities today as compared to a century ago, there are also many stark differences. The culture, heritage and lore of deer camp constantly evolve as the world continues to change.

The grand tradition of deer camp is filled with rituals, customs and anomalies. Some of the larger deer camps of yesteryear in the Northeast and Upper Midwest saw their members coming and going during the November (and sometimes into December) deer season. Like today, many isolated camps were visited on a year-around basis. There were work days in spring, fishing trips in summer and "gettin' ready" days in early fall when the cabins were aired out, leaky roofs and the chinks between logs were repaired, wood was cut for the stove or fireplace, and food and supplies were brought in.

During summer, hunters relished observing red deer in their summer coats and other wildlife as they fished, picked blackberries and enjoyed a few days in their home away from home. Camp members hunted grouse, quail and ducks, small game like rabbits and squirrels, and sometimes set out traps both during the deer season and after.

Come November, opening day was magical. It was comparable to a young boy hoping to find a BB gun under the tree at Christmastime. In fact, many of the adult males in deer camp might easily be accused of reverting back to their boyhood in one way or another. Hunters checked their sights, argued about bullets, shot new rifles for the first time, scouted for sign and prayed for a good tracking snow.

When the shooting actually started, there were plenty of missed shots, blood trails to follow, endless excuses, tall tales and exaggerations about the big ones that got away, and excursions through the snow to help a lucky hunter drag his buck back to camp.

Hunters got snowed in, stuck in the mud, lost in the woods and soaking wet. When they weren't spending agonizing hours sitting by the fire, listening to the rain beat down on the roof of the cabin, they spent miserable hours in the frigid cold and endless wind, praying for the sun to come out and offer a small bit of warmth.

They carried good luck charms into the woods and they named their favorite spots—Beaver Lake, Stag Hill, Buck Ridge, the old salt lick, Blue Springs and Badger Point. They gave each other humorous nicknames—Wrong Way Phil, Sure Shot Al, Sneaky Pete, Ears Murphy.

As Marjorie Williams wrote in her introduction to The Bucks Camp Log—1916-1928, a diary kept by her father and other members of a club in northern Wisconsin published in a book in 1974, "I understand much better what Bucks Camp was all about and I think I know why my father returned from the hunting season bewhiskered and tired, but surely happy as he hung his deer in the garage for all to admire. I know better too why the next November the whole process started all over again."

One thing never changes. With that unfailing optimism possessed by whitetail hunters, a singular, eternal hope is shared by all on the eve of the hunt: tomorrow will be the day I'll get my big buck.

Welcome to the deer woods, my friend!

SOUTHERN COMFORT
A good wall tent that'll keep the mosquitoes out and a well-balanced canoe can come in mighty handy in the southern swamp country. These hunters seem to be contemplating the finer aspects of driving deer with dogs. With his snake leggings and horn to call in the dogs, the mustached gentleman sitting in the middle talks to his companion who holds a shotgun. Several shotguns and a Colt Lightning slide action rifle (probably a .22 for rabbits and turkeys) lean against the tent. The single-shot rifle on the left appears to be an 1885 Browning or Winchester high wall. Laying on the bow of the canoe is an unusual C96 Mauser pistol with a long barrel and rifle stock. With fresh meat in camp—a turkey and two cottontails hanging above the tent opening, supper under the stars will be delightful. Photo circa 1910.

LET THE CELEBRATION BEGIN
 The hunt is over, the Winchesters have proven their worth, and a fine buck has been brought down. Now it's time to open the keg and toast the hunting gods. Photo circa 1925.

THE ESSENCE OF A COZY DEER CAMP
 These hunters stand in front of their cozy cabin as if wanting to invite us inside. What a treat it would be to go back in time and listen to their hunting stories. The man on the right has an early Winchester Model 1894 rifle while his companion standing next to the door wields a Colt Lightning. The man sitting has a lever gun, probably a Winchester as well. Won't you come inside and stay a spell? Photo Upper Midwest, circa 1900.

AHEAD OF THEIR TIME

Two men enjoy the view from a box blind built in a tree deep in a swamp. Although hunting from box blinds and tree stands did not become a common occurrence until decades later, some innovative sports (including market hunters) commonly used home-made tree blinds early in the 20th century. Of course, many a rough-and-ready old deerslayer thought nothing of climbing a tree and toughing it out on a rock-hard limb for long hours at a time. Photo circa 1920.

A 10-POINT BUCK WITH HIS MODEL 10

Hefting a beautiful 10-point buck out of the woods is easy business when you're walking on clouds. This proud hunter has downed a fine buck with his Winchester self-loading Model 1910 semi-automatic. Photo circa 1923.

128 DAWN OF AMERICAN DEER HUNTING

THE BRITISH ARE COMING

These Canadian soldiers appear to have collected a couple of very nice bucks with their old Enfields. Perhaps they are home on leave. The Pattern 1914 Enfield served British and Canadian forces right through World War II and was known for its long-range accuracy as well as its brutal kick. The M1917 Enfield came in .30-06, but it had a red band on the foreground to distinguish it from the 1914 Enfield.

The man at left has a Winchester Model 94. The man next to him is holding a bolt action rifle, while the two men dressed in military attire and the man between them are wielding arm-punishing British Enfields. Photo circa early 1940s.

WELCOME TO THE DEER WOODS

"HOMEWARD BOUND."
Our proud hunter is carrying a Winchester Model 1892 with an octagon barrel and a half magazine. Stereoview Circa 1899.

A HUNTER'S NIGHTMARE
Having shot a doe by mistake with his Winchester Model 94 lever-action rifle during a buck's-only hunt, this disheartened deer slayer is going through the humiliation of losing his deer and paying a fine. It happened during a historic buck hunt in the North Georgia mountains in 1940. Courtesy of *Outdoor Georgia* magazine, October 1941.

INTERVIEW IN THE FIELD
One thousand deer hunters took part in a managed deer hunt conducted in November 1938 in the vast Pisgah National Forest in western North Carolina. Media interest was so keen that CBS radio sent a number of reporters into the woods to interview hunters. The reporters wore red hats and striped shirts for identification and safety. These hunters are being interviewed as they tote a fine eight-point buck out of the woods.

RODE HARD, PUT UP WET!

Standing proudly beside his hefty eight-pointer, this veteran outdoorsman looks like he's definitely been out in the elements for several days. He also appears to be quite resourceful with his venerable Remington Model 8 topped with one of those newfangled telescopic sights. The scope appears to be a turn-of-the-century "Wm. Malcolm" telescopic hunting sight that measures over two feet in length (probably 26 to 28 inches.)

William Malcolm of Syracuse, New York, first made "telescopic lenses" for rifles in 1855, and they became a favorite with both Union and Confederate sharpshooters during the Civil War. Malcolm telescopic sights became popular with some deer hunters in the early 1900s, and the company continued making fine "telescopic lenses for rifles" until just before World War II in 1940. The long 4x or 6x scope seen here was probably side mounted. Photo circa 1915-1920.

Note: If the photo looks familiar, that's because it appeared on the cover of Volume I of *Dawn of American Deer Hunting*. The caption did not run with the photo, so here it is.

TWO BROTHERS, LEARNING HOW TO SHOOT

Looks like dad plans to make sure his two young'uns know how to handle themselves in the deer woods when the time comes. Nothing is more exciting to a boy than learning how to shoot and hunt—especially with dad and their dog. While dad may be taking a few practice shots with his long-barreled Winchester lever-action deer rifle, both brothers appear to be holding single-shot .22 "squirrel guns." The joy of being young . . . If we could only go back in time! Photo 1910.

SUCCESS

A.B. Frost puts us right in the snowy woods alongside these two bear hunters as they take a few moments after the thrill of the hunt to light their pipes and admire their trophy. No doubt those Winchester rifles have also accounted for plenty of venison. Calendar art by A.B. Frost, circa 1895.

132 DAWN OF AMERICAN DEER HUNTING

FIT FOR KINGS
"Home Sweet Home," a back view of a big tent that served as a deer camp deep in the woods. Photo circa 1920.

A glimpse inside the cozy wall tent where it's dry and warm and where deer hunters live like kings. Who could ask for anything more? Note the Adirondack basket pack. Photo circa 1920.

"Trail watching requires patience, something that is somewhat lacking in the hurry and spectacle of modern hunting. And it seems more acceptable to the older, experienced man than it does to the anxious beginner with quick-beating pulse and restless legs. There are not many inveterate trail watchers these days, especially of the old type where the lone hunter seeks to intercept whitetails in their normal daily treks. The numerous hunters in the woods today hamper the natural movements of the animals, and most trail watchers now depend considerably on other hunters to put game past their stands."

George Mattis
Whitetail – Fundamentals and Fine Points for the Hunter (1969)

ANOTHER SMASHING YEAR IN DEER CAMP
This group of proud Pennsylvania hunters has much to celebrate. Their week in deer camp obviously has been exciting, productive and memorable. No location is given for the photo, but it could well have been taken in the Poconos during the mid-to-late 1930s or early 1940s. Most of the deer are youngish bucks, very indicative of a Pennsylvania deer camp during that era.

CHAPTER 9

A METHOD TO THE MADNESS:
DOGS, DEER DRIVES & THE LUCK OF THE IRISH

The mingled destinies of whitetails and men throughout our country's flowered history have seen many ups and downs over the years. When they first reached the shores of the New World, most early English settlers had no idea how to hunt deer and other animals for food. These people typically came from meager backgrounds and had never hunted in the old country. Hunting was a rich man's sport and game populations were tightly controlled. To their ever-lasting credit, local Indians in many areas were very instrumental in teaching early settlers how to hunt and how to use the skins of animals for clothing and other purposes.

After the Pilgrims landed at Plymouth Rock in 1620, over half of the original settlers died within the first 12 months from disease, exposure and starvation. America was a virtual game and fish paradise, yet the Europeans did not know how to take advantage of the endless resources. If it hadn't been for the Indians who gave the Pilgrims food, taught them how to hunt and fish and grow certain crops, the mortality rate no doubt would have been much higher. In fact, the Pilgrims might have perished altogether.

Interestingly, for many years Americans have celebrated "turkey day" as the mainstay of the Thanksgiving Day feast. However, during the first "Thanksgiving" celebration by a grateful group of surviving Pilgrims at Plymouth colony (believed to have taken place in September, 1622), history tells us that the Pokanoket Indians brought five deer to the feast to be shared with the hungry Pilgrims. Although wild turkeys have been associated with our Thanksgiving celebration ever since, those five deer certainly fed a lot more hungry people than the waterfowl and turkeys that were also present at this famous feast.

The new Americans caught on very quickly. Courageous pioneers were soon pushing westward and exploring new frontiers. Hunting deer for food and clothing became part of their daily routines. Whitetails had been the staff of life for the Eastern Indians, and deer soon became almost as important to the new white settlers as well.

The Eastern Indians used an assortment of methods for hunting whitetails. In addition to simply stalking with bows and arrows, they often draped deer skins over their bodies. Acting as human decoys, they were able to sneak very close to feeding deer. Certain tribes also drove deer into bodies of water or into fenced areas, and occasionally employed fire to push deer toward predetermined ambush sites.

With their flintlock firesticks, the settlers employed some of the same methods used by their red brothers, such as driving deer into water where they could be easily killed, usually with large packs of dogs.

Americans loved their dogs, and they quickly realized how beneficial dogs could be. Hunting at night with dogs and fire torches became a favorite strategy.

Hunting at night with a lantern in the front of the canoe became a favored method (see the A.B. Frost print in Chapter 1). The idea was to blind or stun the deer with the light and shoot it as it came down out of the woods to get a drink or feed along the shore line. The lantern gave off just enough light to illuminate the eyes of deer standing close to the shore, and the hunter in the back of the canoe could usually get off a fairly close shot.

In northern climates, hunters learned very quickly how to kill large numbers of deer in heavy snow once the animals yarded up. Market hunters employed this method quite effectively in late winter. The object was to shoot as many deer as possible at any given time. If a hunter saw four deer together, he tried to shoot all four.

The age of market hunting began in the early 1700s from Maine to Florida. In those days, the notion of sportsmanship or fair chase did not exist. Entire herds of deer were slaughtered by market hunters in northern "yarding" areas in deep snow.

As the young country grew and as deer hunting became an annual tradition by

A BOY'S FIRST RIFLE
This illustration could easily be an image of the mustached "old man" presenting "the boy" with his first .22 rifle in Robert Ruark's *The Old Man and the Boy*. Time was when a boy's first rifle was something magical. From BB gun to .22 deer rifle, the exciting progression of a boy learning how to shoot safely and become a deer hunter used to be one of life's most esteemed experiences. Will that tradition continue?

families and ethnic groups in so many places, a transition took place. Laws were passed to protect whitetails and other game animals and different methods of hunting began to evolve. A new deer hunting ethic and the idea of "fair chase" also evolved. Now groups of deer hunters were employing deer drives. The use of dogs was outlawed in many states. Some innovative hunters began employing challenging methods like still-hunting, tracking deer in the snow, or simply finding a good place to sit and watch a deer trail.

Patriotism and deer hunting have always gone hand in hand. That explains why so many policemen, firemen and former military personnel are avid deer hunters.

In the old days, the lucky hunter who was fortunate enough to down a good buck was regaled as a local hero. Sadly, those days are disappearing in many places. But the animal responsible for that kind of excitement is not. He is alive and well and thriving throughout North America.

The root of all hunting revolves around love of country, love of family and patriotism. These days, hunting may be a sweet diversion from the problems of the world. But whatever the method to the madness is, whitetail hunting is always a serious avocation that can never be taken lightly.

A PROUD YOUNG HUNTER
Few deer hunters had the money or the desire to have their trophy whitetails mounted by a competent taxidermist 100 years ago. Most antlers were nailed to the barn wall or used to make knife and fork handles. This young man obviously takes pride in his hunting achievements. In his arms is a tang-sighted Savage Model 1899. Photo circa 1910.

TOTE WHAT YOU SHOOT

The hounds have done their job in the coastal region of eastern North Carolina, and this happy hunter is showing the handler the results of a successful drive. Notice the squirrel tail hanging out of the handler's jacket. Looks like the dogs are ready to go again. Maybe the big one is still out there! Photo November 1944.

THE REDCOATS ARE COMING

Redcoats and hounds equal plenty of venison! The hunting is over, the dogs have done their work, and the meat pole boasts at least two fine bucks, several does and one exceptional bear. It's time to break out the pipes, sit back and reflect. Among this cheerful bunch are several Winchester 94s and several Remington autos. Are the two women visiting wives or camp cooks? Nothing like the camaraderie of deer camp! The presence of deer hounds indicates the photo may be from Virginia or North Carolina, circa late 1950s.

FIVE FOR FIVE

No wonder these satisfied hunters are grinning— five good hunting buddies, five hefty deer on the meat pole. Even the little guy is happy. To be in deer camp with his father and grandfather... How lucky can a growing young'n get? Photo circa 1930.

HUNTER'S DELIGHT IN ONTARIO

The dogs always want to be included in every activity as several men prepare to carry a big doe back to camp on a homemade stretcher. The rifle next to the doe is a Remington Model 14 slide action, while the rifle being held by the man on the left is a Remington Model 25 pump action. Popular cartridges for the Model 25 were the .25-20 and .32-20, both great for small game and considered perfectly adequate for deer. These guns were highly popular with hunters and trappers in Canada and northern tier states in the 1920s and '30s.

There must have been plenty of Scottish blood in the hunters' camp, because the Scottish bagpipes player is preparing to serenade the men in front of their timeless stone clubhouse.

All good things must come to an end. These tired but successful hunters sort their gear and prepare to leave camp with their week's bounty of venison and countless memories that will be with them always. Ontario has long been a sporting paradise to Canadians and Americans alike.

Numerous sportsmen's clubs controlling tens of thousands of acres of prime hunting land date back to the mid to late 1800s. Some were very prestigious in their day. In addition to whitetails, avid American hunters like Theodore Roosevelt traveled to Ontario to hunt caribou (before they were all killed out in southern Ontario), moose and black bears. In their spare time, they participated in outstanding waterfowl hunting and fishing opportunities. C'est la vie! Photos circa 1930s.

Ad for Winchester ammunition, 1949

DEER HUNTING WITH DOGS

Handwritten on the back of this postcard are the words: "Showing how hunters shoot deer hunting with dogs." The photo is too grainy to tell whether or not the older man on left is leaning on a Winchester or Marlin lever-action, but all of the younger men appear to be holding lever guns as well. An airdale, a spaniel and a hound make up quite an assortment of deer dogs. These young men will never forget this memorable day. Photo circa 1915.

LUCKY 13

On the back of this postcard is written: "Snap shots of the Folk Fambly." (The intentional misspelling is likely meant to be humorous). If the Folk family is responsible for all these bucks, they must be outstanding hunters. The hunter appears to be holding a Marlin 1893 lever-action. The popular deer rifle was probably manufactured in the early 1900s. Wonder what the poor folks were doing while this "Folk" and his "Fambly" were out shooting deer. Photo circa 1910.

Judging from the tall lodgepole pines, Mr. Morrison's whitetail camp could well be in Montana or northern Idaho.

HORSE CROSSING CREEK
You can always tell if a deer hunter using a horse is worth his salt because his horse will always have a halter and lead rope placed under the bridle. The halter serves an important function. When the horse (or horses) is tied to a tree for long periods of time while the hunter is out on stand or scouting on foot, the bridle can be removed so that no harm will come to it while the horse is tied out. Photo series circa 1905.

VENISON A'PLENTY
The writing on the back of this cabinet photo identifies the man in the middle as "Tom." The man on the left appears to have a Winchester 1895 in his lap.

MR. MORRISON AND HIS BUCK
With several days' growth of beard, a unique Savage Model 1899F with a rare saddle ring, and his trusty belt knife in a beautifully made sheath, Morrison appears to be a seasoned hunter. That knife will soon be earning its keep. Photo circa 1905.

A GOOD DAY'S HUNT
Mr. Morrison's buck and the Savage Model 1899 Saddle Ring carbine that brought it down. Since he purposely included it in the photo, Mr. Morrison must have been proud of his '99 saddle ring carbine. The rifle was probably made in the early 1900s and may well have been chambered in .303 Savage (the first cartridge designed for the soon-to-be immensely popular Model 99). With some 30 different variations, Savage produced its Model 99s for about 80 years.

"There is a delight in the hardy life of the open. There are no words that can tell the hidden spirit of the wilderness; that can reveal its mystery, its melancholy and its charm. The nation behaves well if it treats the natural resources as assets which it must turn over to the next generation increased and not impaired in value. Conservation means development as much as it does protection."

Theodore Roosevelt 1858-1919

HEAVE HO!

Several game wardens lend assistance to a lucky hunter in loading his trophy buck in the back of the truck. In all, 21 bucks and one doe, shot by mistake, were taken during the 1941 firearms hunt at Blue Ridge WMA. Because the herd had been protected for a number of years, many of the bucks carried outstanding racks. Photo courtesy of the Kenan Research Center at the Atlanta History Center.

CHAPTER 10

MADE IN THE U.S.A.
AMERICA'S NUMBER ONE BIG GAME SENSATION

Arthur Woody was the most famous forest ranger who ever refused to wear a uniform. Born in 1884 near Suches, Georgia, in the heart of Georgia's "high country," legend tells us that he witnessed his father kill the last living deer in Fannin County around 1895 when he was 10 years old. Finally being deemed old enough to go on a hunt with his father and other men from the community, he was beside himself when he was asked to join these much-revered older hunters on his first big hunting adventure. But after his father, Abe Woody, killed what was said to be the last deer in the mountains, young Arthur's elation turned to sadness. It was a life-changing event for the budding hunter.

Certainly the deer Abe Woody killed had to be one of the last deer ever seen in the area during the 19th century. Years later, after Arthur had grown up and gained a reasonable amount of notoriety in his own right, he would immortalize the story by telling people he wholeheartedly believed it was the last deer ever taken in the North Georgia region.

The story soon became a local folk legend, fueled by the fact that as the young mountain boy grew older, he began to nurture a dream that he also shared with a number of people: to one day bring back the beautiful and majestic white-tailed deer that had once been so plentiful in his beloved mountain region.

Sadly, Ranger Woody saw few if any deer in the mountains from 1895 to 1927. He might have stolen a rare glimpse of a straggler from time to time during his wanderings, but for the most part, there were no deer left to see.

Serving as district ranger over many thousands

Arthur Woody, a forest ranger in the North Georgia Mountains from 1918 to 1945, poses with his Savage 99 lever-action rifle chambered in .250-3000 caliber. Like many avid turkey hunters of his day, he preferred a rifle over a shotgun for turkeys. Photo circa 1925.

of acres of North Georgia forestland was not an easy job. It required long hours of hard work and the pay was minimal. But the job did carry a certain amount of prestige. Fortunately, by most pre-Depression standards, the Ranger was fairly well off financially. By 1927 he had done well buying and selling land on the side, and this success gave him a certain amount of financial security. Now he was about to embark on one of the greatest adventures of his life. He was going into the deer-raising business!

"Do what needs to be done and get permission later." That was the Ranger's modus operandi in dealing with his employer, the U.S. Forest Service.

In 1927, the ranger drove to Pisgah National Game Preserve in western North Carolina. He was on a mission. He purchased five young fawns at a reported price of $20 each and took them home. He fed them with a bottle until they were old enough to eat on their own.

Named Nimble, Billy, Nancy, Bessie and Bunny-Girl, the five deer would become the foundation for a growing deer herd that would once again thrive in the North Georgia Mountains. Woody built a pen next to the house to protect the deer from dogs. Nimble and Billy were probably buck fawns, while Nancy, Bessie and Bunny Girl likely were does.

It was reported the deer were so loved by the Woody family that they soon learned how to unlatch the screen door and enter the house. Dick Woody, the ranger's 3-year-old grandson, soon became a favorite playmate of the five. Many a noonday nap was interrupted by his four-legged friends, who could not understand why Dick wasn't playing with them. They would walk into his bedroom and lick his face to wake him.

When the five deer were a year old, they were released inside Rock Creek Refuge (later to become Georgia's first wildlife management area, the Blue Ridge WMA). Once they were free-roaming, Ranger Woody let it be known to one and all that there would be a steep price to pay if anything happened to any of his deer. Over the next few years, he continued buying deer from Pisgah Reserve and releasing them in the refuge. By the late 1930s, the well-protected deer had multiplied to an estimated 2,000 animals.

Because the herd was thriving, sportsmen began to petition the state and the Forest Service to allow some sort of legal hunting. In the fall of 1940, much to the chagrin of Ranger Woody, the first legal deer hunt of modern times was held in the refuge. Twenty-two bucks were taken by delighted hunters.

Ranger Arthur Woody had grown up hunting turkeys and small game, but he had never hunted deer because they had been absent from the mountains during his early years. Now these deer had become like children to him, and he was adamantly against any type of hunting. But the tough old mountain man had to relinquish his feelings and he did. Outwardly, he praised the hunters as they brought their trophies into the check station. Inwardly, he was greatly saddened because many of the bucks he knew by name.

After his death in 1946, Arthur Woody became widely known as the "Barefoot Ranger of Suches." He left behind a legacy of conservation and humanitarian achievements that is unmatched in Georgia history. Today he is best known for his work in reintroducing deer to the mountain region.

This story is just one example of the amazing impact white-tailed deer have had on numerous individuals throughout our country's colorful history. Truly, whitetails are America's No. 1 big game sensation.

A UNIQUE SUCCESS STORY: THE WINDS OF WAR

As noted in the feature on the previous pages, Ranger Arthur Woody (1884-1946, pictured second from left) was the man responsible for bringing deer back to the North Georgia mountains. By 1900, deer had disappeared from the mountain region as a result of over-hunting by hungry pioneers and homesteaders. Woody began restocking deer in 1927. By 1940, his well-protected herd had burgeoned to an estimated 2,000 animals in the recently established Blue Ridge WMA, Georgia's first wildlife management area and one of the first in the nation. Due to a growing demand by sportsmen, state and officials of the U.S. Forest Service worked in unison to sanction the first managed deer hunt of the 20th century in Ranger Woody's beloved refuge. The hunt took place in the fall of 1940. Twenty-two bucks were killed during that historic inaugural hunt.

The following year, a second hunt was held in which 21 bucks were tagged. Because of the level of public interest, both the 1940 and 1941 hunts were high-profile media events, and Ranger Arthur Woody became a national celebrity. At the time the 1941 hunt was held in November of that year, no one could have predicted the events of December 7, only a few short weeks away. The surprise attack on Pearl Harbor turned the world upside down and changed an innocent nation forever. Despite the horrors to come over the next four years, deer hunting remained one of America's most steadfast pastimes for those individuals fortunate enough to remain at home.

PROUD OF HIS DAD

The budding deer hunter on the right is no doubt very proud of his dad, and Dad is no doubt equally proud of the outstanding trophy buck he bagged during the November 1941 hunt at Blue Ridge WMA in the North Georgia mountains. The game warden admires the beautiful 8-pointer downed with a 1903 Springfield .30-06, used by the military during World War I and soon to be used in the Second World War as well. Sadly, the U. S. would be forced to enter World War II only a few short weeks after this photo was taken. Photo courtesy of the Kenan Research Center at the Atlanta History Center.

Ad for Marlin lever-action rifles, 1949

THE SMILE SAYS IT ALL
Two elated hunters congratulate each other after participating in the hunt of a lifetime. Years of hard work and time were invested by Ranger Arthur Woody and the U. S. Forest Service in protecting and growing the Blue Ridge deer herd in order to reach this high point in November 1941. Photo courtesy of the Kenan Research Center at the Atlanta History Center.

BLUE RIDGE BUCKS
Two proud hunters smile for the camera as they show off their Blue Ridge bucks, the one on the right being a magnificent 10-pointer. The hunter on the left is holding a Winchester Model 1873 lever-action (manufactured from 1873 to 1923), while his partner wields an ever-popular Remington Model 25 pump. Both guns were highly desired deer rifles in the early 1900s. They might well be old heirlooms passed down from father to son and taken out of mothballs for this special hunt. Photo circa 1941, courtesy of the Kenan Research Center at the Atlanta History Center.

RELAXING IN THE DEER WOODS
Well-known political leader and diplomat Adlai Stevenson II takes a few days off to participate in a deer hunt with dogs near Aberdeen, North Carolina in the Sandhills region in November, 1954. Stevenson served as governor of Illinois from 1949 to 1953 and made three unsuccessful bids for president in 1952, 1956 and 1960. After John Kennedy was elected president in 1960, Stevenson served as ambassador to the United Nations from 1961 to 1965.

"THE LIFE I LOVE."
This bustling deer camp is probably tucked away somewhere in the Adirondacks. Although the four seasoned woodsmen seem to be taking a mid-day break, a lot is going on in front of this remote cabin in the woods. One good buck is hanging, possibly the result of the morning hunt. Snowshoes hang on the side of the cabin just in case of bad weather. The dogs are resting on blankets in the snow. No doubt they'll be taking up the trail again on the afternoon hunt. Several of the long guns are muzzle-loading shotguns, but the second man from the right is holding a newfangled Winchester or Marlin lever-action. Photo by B.W. Kilburn, Littleton, NH, circa 1888.

LAST DAY LUCK
(WISCONSIN RAPIDS *DAILY TRIBUNE*)

Longbow hunter Fred Shane of St. Louis Park, Minnesota earned his deer the hard way. Hunting just north of Grantsburg, Wisconsin, he devoted 41 days out of the 45-day archery season to pursuing whitetails. Finally, on the last day of the 1950 archery season, he scored a perfect shot on this fine doe. He was stalk-hunting on the ground when he arrowed this deer.

LIVING THE DREAM

What can be more American than bagging a nice buck out in the hinterlands and getting it safely home in a durable 1925 Chevrolet touring car? Photo circa late 1920s.

ONLY IN AMERICA

Baseball, apple pie, Chevrolet and a good white-tailed buck on the hood. God bless this great land! Photo circa 1950.

A HOME RUN IN THE DEER WOODS

Well-known baseball player Ted Williams (1918-2002) was a six-foot, four-inch slugging sensation and avid sportsman who hit 521 home runs during his stellar career. And that was after taking time off to go and fight in two wars. Named after Theodore Roosevelt, he played his entire 19-year Major League baseball career as a left fielder for the Boston Red Sox from 1939 to 1960. His career was twice interrupted when he served his country during World War II and the Korean War. Beginning in 1943, he served three years in the U.S. Navy and Marine Corps as an aviator during World War II. He returned to active military duty for portions of 1952 and 1953 to serve as a Marine combat aviator in the Korean War. Williams was the last player in Major League Baseball history to attain a batting average of over .400, hitting .406 in 1941. He retired as an active player in 1960.

Like many sports figures, Williams was an avid outdoorsman all his life. He was a dedicated fly fisherman and hosted a TV program about fishing. He was inducted into the International Game Fish Association Hall of Fame in 2000. He loved saltwater fishing but he was also an avid deer hunter. After his retirement from baseball, he served a number of years as a popular spokesperson for Sears Roebuck, endorsing several lines of hunting, fishing and baseball equipment. Photo circa 1955.

BASEBALL, APPLE PIE AND DEER HUNTING

Born in Starkville, Mississippi in 1903, Thomas "Cool Papa" Bell (right) was a gifted outfielder who played in the Negro League. He played on various teams from 1922 to 1946. He started out with the St. Louis Stars as a left-handed pitcher but injured his arm and moved to the outfield. He was said to be the fastest man who ever played the game. In one 200-game season, he reportedly stole 175 bases. "Cool Papa" played on three of the greatest teams in the history of black baseball: the St. Louis Stars, the Pittsburgh Crawfords and the Homestead Grays. Bell was elected to the Baseball Hall of Fame in 1974. He died in 1991.

Pictured here with a hunting companion the year after he retired as a player in 1947, Cool Papa is brandishing a Remington Model 141. Judging by the license plate on the Oldsmobile, the two men were probably hunting in Pennsylvania.

REMINGTON MODEL 141

An upgrade version of the popular Model 14, the Remington Model 141 "Gamemaster" pump-action repeating rifle was introduced in 1935. Some 75,000 rifles were made from 1935 to 1951. Interestingly, the original Model 14 was designed by John Pedersen because Remington wanted to produce a rifle that would compete with the Winchester '94 lever action. For some reason, however, Remington decided not to offer the 141 in the two most popular calibers of the day, the .30-30 and .300 Savage. This ultimately hurt sales. Instead, it was offered in the same three calibers as the Model 14: .30 Remington, .32 Remington and .35 Remington. The rifle's design did offer several innovative features, one being a spiral magazine tube that prevented the bullet tips from contacting the primer of the cartridge in front of them. The magazine moved with the fore-end when pumping the action. Loading was through an opening in the magazine itself. In the late 1930s, the Model 141 sold for about $46.

"God intended women to be outside as well as men and they do not know what they are missing when they stay cooped up in the house. Any woman who does not thoroughly enjoy tramping across the country on a clear frosty morning with a good gun and a pair of dogs does not know how to enjoy life."

Annie Oakley
1860-1926

THE WINCHESTER GIRLS

These refined ladies seem to be taking their deer hunting very seriously. Were these extraordinary bucks the result of their skills and true aim, or are these members of the fairer sex proudly posing with the handiwork of their menfolk? The young lady on the right seems to clearly answer the question. With her Winchester Model 94 and a buck that would be the envy of every deer hunter in the state, she is telling the camera her magic bullet did the deed. The rifle on the left appears to be a Winchester as well, while the lady in white is holding a rifle that cannot be distinguished. One thing is certain. This was one unforgettable hunt! Photo circa 1912.

CHAPTER 11

THE GIRLS OF AUTUMN:
FROM PETTICOATS TO SMOKING RIFLES

Archaeological evidence from prehistoric times teaches us that, thousands of years ago, women were worshiped by various cultures as goddesses. In early hunter-gatherer societies, women were held in high esteem because they were thought to have magical powers. Women were capable of doing things men could never do. Women were the givers of life and the bearers of children. Men of the tribe provided food through hunting and they protected the women and children from any outside dangers, but there was nothing magical about what they did.

In Roman mythology, Diana was the much revered goddess of the hunt. She was often depicted in various artforms holding a bow and arrow, the weapon of the day for the Romans and Greeks, and a deer would often appear in the scene with her. Diana was associated with wild animals and the woodlands. She had the power to talk to animals and held control over them. She was also the virgin goddess of the moon and childbirth, being equated with the Greek goddess Artemis. As a maiden goddess, she could never marry.

Over the course of history, the macho male slowly replaced the goddess as an object of worship. In more modern times, the male has usually been depicted as the hero of the hunt, although American women have made great contributions to our hunting heritage for several centuries.

Throughout our nation's colorful 400-year history, whenever the going got tough, the so-called "weaker sex" was always right there alongside their men doing whatever needed to be done. As the country expanded and steadily moved westward, women played a key role in building homesteads, tending to their families and even protecting them from harm.

Many frontier women were better rifle shots than their husbands. While the men were away on business, women sometimes had to fight hostile Indians and deal with prairie fires, flash floods and stampeding buffalo. They worked in the garden, prepared food, took care of the livestock and made clothing. In their spare time, they often went out and shot a deer or a couple of prairie chickens for the pot. Women have been skilled hunters for generations. And through it all, they've never lost their femininity and lady-like charm.

Annie Oakley always dressed like a lady and made every effort to appear feminine and ladylike in public. She believed it was every woman's job to act like a woman. Even though she performed at what many regarded as a "man's job," she made every effort to always act like a lady. The same is true with Mary Augusta "Gusty" Wallihan, who you'll meet in the next few pages. Gusty lived on the frontier, hunted alongside her husband and became a noted wildlife photographer, but she always dressed like a lady, even when she was stalking wild animals with her camera. Gusty might have worn a petticoat, but like Annie Oakley, she certainly knew how to shoot a rifle!

ANNIE OAKLEY QUAIL HUNTING IN NORTH CAROLINA
In order to put food on the table for her mother and siblings, Annie Oakley killed her first deer in Ohio when she was age 10. By the time she was 13, she was so proficient at hunting whitetails that she began selling venison and small game to local grocers. In addition to her incredible shooting skills, she had a lifelong love for hunting deer, small game and birds. After retiring from show business in the early 1900s, she and her husband Frank Butler spent much time hunting quail, ducks and other small game in North Carolina and Florida. Photo circa 1920. (See Chapter 15 for more about Annie Oakley).

THE RIGHT RIFLE

This photo appeared on page 186 in the first volume of *Dawn of American Deer Hunting*. The 250-pound bruiser was killed by high school senior Catherine Turner of Windsorville, Maine on November 24, 1938. In the caption describing the photo, I mistakenly identified the rifle Catherine was using as a long barreled Winchester Model 94. The gun is, in fact, a Marlin 1892 lever-action, although the distinct V-shaped metal screw housing at the top of the lever is difficult to see. Believe me, I heard about my mistake from a number of readers across the country, including the editor of *American Hunter* magazine. I decided to use this great photo again so that my transgression could be rectified.

BIG SKY PRIZE

Internationally acclaimed New York Metropolitan Opera soprano Mona Paulee (1911-1995), who possessed an incredible voice, smiles broadly over her first whitetail buck taken near Kalispell, Montana in December 1946. Pictured with her husband, Dean Holt, she's holding a mid-1940s Savage 99, probably a .300, equipped with a peep sight.

A former pilot in the Army Transport Command during World War II and popular band leader before the war, Mona's dedicated husband often flew her to numerous post-war singing engagements across the country in his Beech Bonanza. The couple prided themselves in never missing a single appearance, and Holt often played the piano during his wife's performances. The Montana hunt was no doubt a memorable experience for the adventurous couple. Photo circa 1946.

MODERN-DAY ROBIN HOODS
The art of hunting for whitetails with archery tackle was still in its infancy when longbow hunters Mr. and Mrs. Fred Thompson of Atlanta, GA participated in a much-publicized 1940 archery deer hunt held on national forest land at the Blue Ridge Wildlife Management Area in the North Georgia mountains. Conducted jointly by the U.S. Forest Service and the Georgia Wildlife Commission, this was the first managed deer hunt in the mountain region of the 20th century. It took several more seasons before the Thompsons tagged their first bow-killed bucks. Photo 1940.

This life-size sculpture of Goddess/Huntress Diana riding a deer resembles a large whitetail doe. The statue is located in an elaborate garden or park, likely somewhere in Europe.

Discovered in Italy, the original marble stature of Goddess Diana reaching for an arrow now resides in the Louvre Museum in Paris.

THAT FEMININE TOUCH

After five years of deer hunting with no success, Mrs. H. L. Ripley of Cadiz, Ohio ventured out to Jefferson County near East Springfield on opening day of Ohio's 1953 deer season. Twelve minutes into the young season, this magnificent 10-pointer appeared and she knew what to do. Her husband had gone to Pennsylvania to hunt that day. Empty handed, he returned home to a freezer full of venison.

"THE FEMALE DEER SLAYERS OF THE ADIRONDACKS."

It was not uncommon for refined ladies from cities like Boston and New York to accompany their husbands to deer camp in the Adirondacks in the early 20th century and "outhunt" the menfolk. The rifle on the left is an 1886 Colt "Lightning" Medium Frame Slide Action, originally chambered in .44-40. The lever-action carbine on the right appears to be a Winchester Model 1892. Stereoview by American Photo Company, Ilion, New York. Circa early 1900s.

ONE SHOT WAS ALL SHE NEEDED
Best known for its shotguns, the Syracuse Arms Co. of Syracuse, New York produced firearms between 1888 and 1908. This refined lady certainly knew how to handle a 16-gauge. Circa 1903.

A LADY AND HER DEER

Among many other skills, pioneer women were often excellent rifle shots. The well-dressed lady pictured with this outstanding mule deer buck is Mary Augusta "Gusty" Wallihan. Born in Wisconsin in 1837, Gusty and her family migrated west. She ended up living in western Colorado with her brother Thomas. In 1885, she married Allen Wallihan, 22 years her junior. The couple settled near Rawlings, Wyoming.

Gusty later wrote: "My brother and Mr. Wallihan wanted me to learn to shoot. We were miles from any house — alone in the mountains. I had fired a revolver a few times and a gun once. The men had plans for me to use our Parker shotgun on cottontail rabbits. When I made my first attempt, I could not hold the shotgun out at arm's length, so I learned to shoot from a rest. After a short time, I tried a shot off-hand at some geese flying over and killed one at 60 yards and about 75 feet high, which surprised and pleased my brother and Mr. W. and myself as well. My first deer I got next spring, shooting him in the neck, dropping him."

Gusty later killed two deer with one shot. Even when she was out hunting, Gusty always dressed like a lady. The more time she spent chasing deer and other game animals, the more she began to think about photographing local wildlife. She acquired a camera through a trade and began taking wildlife photos with Allen. Over the next 10 years, the couple took hundreds of outstanding and historic wildlife photos. They became nationally known, publishing two books of photographs: *Hoofs, Claws and Antlers of the Rocky Mountains*, published in 1894, and *Camera Shots at Big Game*, published in 1901. Theodore Roosevelt wrote introductions for both books. Gusty died in 1922 after suffering a stroke. Photo circa 1895.

SNOWY, SNOWY DAY

A brave young lady and her husband have just emerged from the warmth of the cabin and are ready to face the elements. She is holding a Winchester Model 10 in .401 caliber and a four-shot magazine. He is holding what appears to be an early Savage 99. What will the afternoon hold? Photo circa 1920.

FOR THE LOVE OF HUNTING

Mrs. Julia Hagenauer, 63, proudly stands beside the young buck and black bear she shot on Nov. 23, 1950 near Munising, Michigan with her lever-action .30-30. Mrs. Hagenauer had been an avid hunter for over 20 years.

ALL THE COMFORTS OF HOME

The "strenuous life" of camping out and chasing big game often written about by Theodore Roosevelt builds a powerful appetite. There is no better way to give deer camp that "home away from home" atmosphere than to start the day with a tasty bowl of Kellogg's Toasted Corn Flakes, a bowl of oat meal and a cup of hot black coffee. With one buck already hanging in camp, this proud huntress is holding her pump-action Remington Model 25 (possibly a .25-20). Perhaps she is contemplating the afternoon hunt. Note the two Winchesters leaning nearby. Wilderness living certainly has its appeal. Photo circa 1920.

GIRL WITH A GRIZZLY

Holding her dependable bolt-action rifle, this attractive and adventurous young lady stands proudly in front of her immense brown bear skin, probably taken in Alaska. Photo circa 1935.

A BIG GUN FOR THE LITTLE LADY

Not to be outdone by the menfolk, this sophisticated lady has grabbed a shotgun loaded with buckshot and ventured away from the lodge to a spot where she hopes a big buck will happen by. And who knows? She might well outhunt her husband and the other men in camp. Photo taken in the Adirondacks, circa 1905.

"I hunt deer because I love the entire process; the preparations, the excitement, and sustained suspense of trying to match my woodslore against the finely honed instincts of these creatures. On most days spent in the woods, I come home with an honestly earned feeling that something good has taken place. It makes no difference whether I got anything; it has to do with how the day was spent."

Fred Bear
From an article by Dr. Rob Wegner
Titled, "The Man with the Borsalino Hat"

HIS GREATEST PASSION
Yes this is Theodore Roosevelt, posing for the camera after a successful mountain lion hunt out West. No former president in American history was more passionate about big game hunting and no president has done more for conservation and wildlife. (See Chapter 15 for more on Theodore Roosevelt.) Photo circa later 1890s.

CHAPTER 12

MIXED BAG:
LURE OF THE WILDERNESS (OTHER SPECIES)

For most hunters of yesteryear who spent a week or longer in deer camp, the ultimate goal was to have a good whitetail buck hanging on the meat pole. But the range of other big game species, including moose and black bears, often over-lapped into whitetail country, and hunters were sometimes rewarded with an unanticipated trophy.

In the late 1800s, woodland caribou were still present in northern Maine and parts of the Upper Midwest. Sadly, the caribou were all killed out in Maine and along the northern fringes of Michigan, Minnesota and Wisconsin by the early 1900s, and they never made a comeback. With such a wide distribution, black bears and turkeys (considered to be big game) were perhaps the most abundant species in the whitetail woods.

Moose were also found in reasonable numbers in the Upper Midwest and many areas in the Northeast. A moose added to the meat pole was a bonus in any deer camp. Wolves were not uncommon in the Upper Midwest and northern plains, but they were always a challenge to kill. Being offered a shot at one of these ghosts of the woods was considered a gift from heaven for most whitetail hunters. Some states paid bounties on wolves well into the early 20th century.

In parts of Montana, Idaho and the Dakotas, mule deer, elk, mountain lions, moose, black bears, grizzlies, wolves and sometimes even a stray antelope might find its way into whitetail country. In some areas it was not uncommon for a whitetail hunter to shoot a mule deer buck and a whitetail buck on the same day

The vast majority of avid whitetail hunters were content to go to deer camp year after year with friends and family and spend each season chasing whitetails. The lure of the wilderness held a strong appeal to these hunters, and if they happened to shoot a bear or a moose, they viewed it as a blessing in disguise.

But some hunters hitched their wagons to a different star. Men like Theodore Roosevelt and George Custer, featured in Chapter 15, hunted many other species of North American big game (or in Roosevelt's case, game in other parts of the world).

Custer's Army career on the plains after the Civil War in the late 1860s and early '70s happened to coincide with the last years of the great buffalo migrations before the herds were wiped out. To him, stalking buffalo was the pinnacle of all big game hunting. He went on numerous bison hunts, and he brought back plenty of buffalo meat.

A decade later in the mid-1880s when Roosevelt reached the Dakota Territory, the vast herds of buffalo were nearly gone, but he was able to find and shoot a few stragglers.

Like Roosevelt and Custer, men constantly seeking adventure and new horizons in their lives would always be looking over the next hill, but they never forgot their whitetail roots. A prolific writer, Roosevelt wrote fondly about his whitetail hunting experiences in North Dakota. Custer never got the chance to write about some of his early hunting experiences. Although he did a fair amount of writing about his hunting exploits on the plains, he never lived long enough to write about his early days of whitetail hunting as a boy in Michigan. Custer was only 36 when he died.

A HARLEY AND A LONG BOW
This modern-day Robin Hood has answered the call of adventure. Using his Harley to go places where no man has dared venture before, he has slain a mighty black bear with a wooden arrow from his longbow somewhere in the wilds of Michigan. His Maid Marion should be duly impressed. Photo circa early 1940s.

A LUCKY WOLF HUNTER
Wielding a Winchester Model 1895 (possibly a takedown), this proud hunter appears to be snowshoeing across a frozen lake as he heads back to camp with his prize of a lifetime, a thick-coated timber wolf. At the time this photo was taken in the early 1900s, wolves were considered vermin in many Midwestern states and some of them offered bounties. Bounty or no, it was always a thrill for a deer hunter to shoot a wolf! Photo circa 1910.

"ONE GOOD SHOT DID THE WORK: BEAR HUNTING IN WYOMING, U.S.A."
This happy hunter poses with his Savage 1899 and his prize of the day. Stereoview from Underwood and Underwood, 1904.

BABE THE HUNTER

Yes this is the Babe with a big turkey gobbler. When he wasn't blasting home runs out of the ball park, George Herman "Babe" Ruth (1895-1948) loved nothing better than to spend time outdoors. In addition to his love for golf, he was an avid hunter and fisherman. Nicknamed the "Bambino" and the "Sultan of Swat," Ruth's baseball career spanned 22 seasons from 1914 through 1938. He started out as a left-handed pitcher for the Boston Red Sox, but soon made a name for himself as one of baseball's greatest hitters. He slugged 714 home runs and won seven World Series, four with the New York Yankees. With his great fame and outgoing personality, he was frequently invited to New England and southern Ontario on deer and bear hunts. He also shot geese, turkeys and small game in numerous eastern states. Ruth was elected into the Baseball Hall of Fame in 1936. Believed by many to be the greatest baseball player of all time, Babe Ruth died of cancer at age 53 in 1948. Photo circa 1940.

BOY BEAR-SLAYER

Judging by the look on his face and the way he's holding his rifle, there can be little doubt this young man has just joined the brotherhood of mighty bear slayers. The proud man on the left is probably his father. The versatile old Savage '99, likely his dad's, has done it again. Photo circa 1910.

A FINE GOBBLER

If you had a nickel for every wild turkey or deer taken with a Stevens single-shot (or double-barrel) 12- or 16-gauge shotgun in the last 100 years you'd be a wealthy man. This proud hunter poses with a fine gobbler taken with his shoulder-punishing 12-gauge. Looks like he might have a few notches on the stock of his gun. Photo circa 1910.

STEVENS SHOTGUNS

Among their many other popular guns, J. Stevens and Co. began producing single-barreled shotguns in 1872. The original Model 30 came in 14-gauge but the company soon offered 10, 12, 16, and 20 gauge as well. Stevens produced its first double barreled shotgun in 1876. Available in 10 and 12 gauge, it had three triggers, the third used to unlock the action. Between 1900 and 1916, Stevens produced 26 single-barreled shotgun models.

GREAT DAY TO BE ALIVE!
 Rabbit hunting doesn't get much better than this. As they cheerfully head home through the snow with their day's bounty of cottontails, these energetic souls know they have created some special memories, especially for the youngest member of the family who proudly holds his own rabbit. What a way to spend a day! Photo circa 1950s.

"NEARING HOME WITH OUR SHARE OF THE WEEK'S WORK."
Stereoviews by Underwood and Underwood, 1894. This caribou hunt probably took place in southern Ontario near the Minnesota/Canada border. Stereoviews circa 1894.

CARIBOU HUNT
"That's where I hit him." "C'est la je l'ai touché !"

MIXED BAG, LURE OF THE WILDERNESS (OTHER SPECIES)

Ernest Hemingway's father, Dr. Clarence "Ed" Hemingway, poses with a black bear hide and whitetail antlers taken while hunting in the Great Smoky Mountains of North Carolina in 1891. A love of hunting and outdoor adventure ran deep in the Hemingway family. The elder Hemingway is holding a long-barreled percussion mountain rifle probably made in the Carolinas or Tennessee by a backwoods gunmaker.

Ernest holds a crow he shot in 1913 with his father's lever-action Winchester Model 1887 shotgun.

Both photos courtesy of the Ernest Hemingway Collection at the John F. Kennedy Presidential Library, Boston.

THE SPORTING LIFE OF ERNEST HEMINGWAY

During his early years, acclaimed author Ernest Hemingway spent many halcyon days at his family's Windemere cabin in northwestern Michigan. It was there between 1900 and 1918 that he developed his love of hunting and wild places—passions he would pursue throughout the remainder of his life. It was also where he developed his unique writing style that would culminate with the Pulitzer Prize for his book, The Old Man and the Sea.

Right: Ernest (left) and his friend Harold Sampson carefully tote a porcupine they shot after it had quilled the neighbor's dog. Young Ernest is carrying a single-barreled 20-gauge given to him for his 10th birthday by his paternal grandfather, Anson Hemingway. Ernest's father firmly believed that any wild creature killed by a hunter must be eaten. So, that evening, Ernest's mother cooked the porcupine haunches for hours, but they still tasted like shoe leather, Hemingway recalls. Photo courtesy of the Ernest Hemingway Collection at the John F. Kennedy Presidential Library, Boston.

Below: Ernest Hemingway takes a shot with his favorite rifle, a .30-06 Springfield 03-actioned rifle built exclusively for him by Griffin & Howe in New York. Upon receiving the rifle, Hemingway removed the scope and shot all of his game with the open sights.

HOLLYWOOD HUNTERS

Hollywood heartthrobs Carole Lombard (1908-1942) and Clark Gable (1901-1960) smile as they show off a handful of South Dakota pheasants. Lombard was said to be the love of Gable's life. The couple married in March 1939 and shared a few happy years together before Lombard died in a plane crash in 1942 while on a tour selling war bonds. She was 33. Gable was devastated and enlisted in the army.

During their short time together, the inseparable couple lived on a small ranch in California. The outgoing and boisterous Lombard loved to accompany the low-key Gable on his hunting, fishing and shooting excursions. Photo circa 1940.

LEGENDARY OUTDOOR WRITER

Jack O'Connor (1902-1978) poses with an exceptional Dall ram and a bull elk. As the longtime gun editor of *Outdoor Life* magazine, O'Connor traveled the world hunting big game and writing columns, stories and books about his exploits. He was a great proponent of the .270 round for many big game species, including whitetails. His hands-down favorite big game animals were the four species of North American sheep. Photos courtesy Buck Buckner; circa late 1950s.

WORLDLY HUNTER
Eleanor O'Connor hunted with husband, Jack, throughout North America and even in India and Africa. Behind her is a forkhorn mule deer she took with her Remington 30S in .257 Roberts. Jack killed the larger buck with his Mauser 7x57. They were hunting from Moquitch Camp in the Kaibab of north-central Arizona. Photo courtesy Buck Buckner.

"PERILS OF THE WILDERNESS – A FIGHT FOR LIFE"
One hunter raises an ax as the big bruin bites into the hand of the knife-wielding man on the ground. Note the victim's broken (disassembled) shotgun on the ground. Attacks like this certainly happened in real life, and as stereoviews became more popular in the late 1800s, companies like Underwood and Underwood loved to embellish scenes depicting danger and drama. Stereoview by Underwood and Underwood, 1893.

FOUND TREASURE

This somewhat weathered moose skull was probably found while these men were whitetail hunting. The man on the left, probably the guide, is holding a half-magazine Winchester Model 1892. The older gentleman on the right also has what appears to be a lever-action Winchester. Although plenty of yesteryear's big game hunters specifically went after moose in the North Country of the U.S. and in southern Canada, most whitetail hunters operating in moose country seldom encountered one of the big deer. In most whitetail camps, to shoot a moose was icing on the cake. Photo circa 1905.

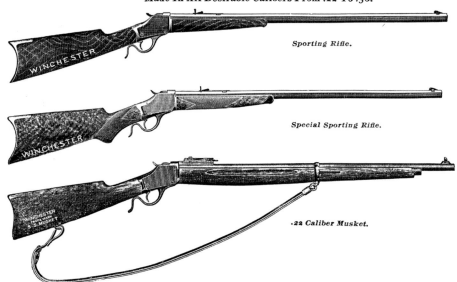

MIXED BAG, LURE OF THE WILDERNESS (OTHER SPECIES)

BOBCAT HUNTER
"A Cat That Never Awoke After My Gun Spoke – Incident of a Wild Cat Hunt in Colorado, U.S.A." Note the large horn the hunter has around his shoulder, probably used for calling his dogs. Stereoview from the Keystone View Company, 1903.

A MESS OF BUSHYTAILS
Many a youngster growing up in the early 1900s cut his teeth hunting small game before he graduated to deer. Numerous are the stories about Depression-era boys who were told by their father, "Son, here's one shell. Take the shotgun and go out and shoot something for supper." That "something" was in all likelihood a squirrel or a rabbit, maybe a quail or dove. If that boy was extraordinarily lucky, he might get two quail or doves with one shot. Squirrels and rabbits were common table fare during the tough times in the 1920s leading up to the Great Depression and in the years prior to World War II. Boys who could handle a shotgun, or "bark" a squirrel off a limb with a .22 rifle, grew up to become very proficient deer hunters. Photo circa 1925.

TWO GOOD GOATS

George "Coyote" Smith poses with a pair of Wyoming antelope, known locally as "goats," taken on Deer Creek with his Model 1873 Winchester. Smith was a well-known character and Jack-of-all-trades in late-19th-century Wyoming. After several failed business attempts, he began hunting coyotes in the Lander area around 1898. At the time, prime hides brought up to $1 each. In addition to coyotes, Smith hunted and trapped wolves, bobcats, deer, antelope and other small game. His wife, Hattie, made coats out of bobcat skins, and the couple soon prospered from their work. Smith was also a talented photographer and operated a studio in Glenrock for a time. He took many historic photos, and later served a stint as Glenrock's town marshal, newspaper editor and postmaster. Photo circa 1898.

MOUNTAIN MAN IN GOD'S COUNTRY

He was a mighty hunter before the Lord; therefore it is said, "like Nimrod the mighty hunter before the Lord."
Genesis X, 9

MIXED BAG, LURE OF THE WILDERNESS (OTHER SPECIES)

CONTEMPLATING THE HUNT
This satisfied hunter has every reason to be pleased. The Marlin has spoken, the shot was well placed and the trophy hangs next to the cabin. Even though the young muley has a small rack, he's a trophy in every way to this satisfied hunter, and the memory of the day's adventure will forever be etched in his mind. Probably manufactured in the early 1900s, his rifle of choice is a Model 1893 Marlin lever-action with a standard 24-inch round barrel, pistol grip stock and half-length tube magazine. The knee-high, World War I-style leather boots may indicate our hunter is a veteran of the trenches. Photo circa 1925.

A WELL-SPENT DAY
A good horse, a good dog and a good rifle: What else could a contented man ask for? The old Winchester '92 has proven its worth once again, and this proud hunter is returning to the homestead with a fine young mule deer buck in velvet. Did the dog take part in the chase? Photo circa 1890.

WYOMING DANDY

Okay, so this young man is a bit of a showoff. He obviously has the world by the tail. With a fine steed, a good rifle, a pistol on his hip and the results of several days' efforts out on the prairie, he seemingly has made easy work in collecting these prime pelts. No wonder he's feeling invincible. You can't knock success. The rifle appears to be some type of rolling block single-shot in a small caliber. With his skills, maybe this young man should think about signing on with Buffalo Bill's Wild West Show. Photo believed to have been taken in central Wyoming, circa later 1890s.

A TRAPPING TRIO

Trapping beaver and other furry critters in the cold North Country often went hand in hand with whitetail hunting. Maybe that's why the gentleman on the left is brandishing one of those revolutionary new Winchester Model 1907 self-loading take-downs. It'll handle anything the North Country has to offer! Photo circa 1915.

"As a youngster, I was always greatly mystified and awed by this November ritual of deer hunting and the inevitable exodus to Bucks Camp. Several weeks before the event took place, my father began to acquire a kind of glow and the smell of gun oil and rubber boots hung in the air. An object referred to as a pack sack was brought forth filled with wool socks, flannel shirts and, more to the point, a big bar of German sweet chocolate for quick energy in case he got lost in the woods.

"I knew what happened on the home front while the men were off on this hunting foray. My mother locked more doors than usual, we got to sleep later and all the neighborhood women and children gathered for a manless Thanksgiving Dinner."

From *The Bucks Camp Log*, edited by Marjorie Williams, 1974

LIKE FATHER, LIKE SON
With their Jeep in the background and a pair of bolt-action rifles, a smiling father and a beaming son proudly show off their bounty. It's a good bet this young man will never forget the memories made on this special day in the woods with his dad. Photo early 1960s.

CHAPTER 13

A THOUSAND CAMPFIRES AGO

There was a time when city and country newspapers featured front-page stories with photos about outstanding bucks taken by lucky hunters. There was a time when country inns and restaurants openly welcomed deer hunters to stay and eat at their establishments and put out signs saying "Deer Hunters Welcome." There was a time when small town diners would open at 4 a.m. to cater to early-rising deer hunters who needed some strong coffee and a good breakfast under their belts before they invaded the woods. These diners became social gathering hubs and staging areas for the armies of plaid and checkered "redcoats" who would soon be braving the cold and hoping to fill a deer tag.

There was a time when schools closed on opening day of deer season in some communities so that long-standing family traditions involving fathers and sons, grandfathers and uncles, cousins and nephews could be carried out in remote deer camps. There was a time when handing down an heirloom shotgun or rifle like a vintage Winchester 1895 to a son or grandson that Grandpa had used to waylay so many fine whitetail bucks over the years was a time-honored family ritual and much-cherished tradition.

There was a time when deer hunters were considered to be unique individuals indeed, men of nature who were fiercely independent and marched to a different drummer.

Like the animal he hunted, the true whitetail hunter of yesteryear was a conglomeration of many things. First and foremost, he was a knowledgeable woodsman and naturalist. Experience taught him how to read the woods like he read the morning newspaper. Nothing went unnoticed. He had an intimate knowledge of deer sign, animal behavior, body language and the haunts where deer lived. Some hunters who were really good at what they did even possessed a self-developed intuition or "sixth sense." This instinctive intuition helped them make the right move in many instances during the ultimate chess game with a most challenging opponent.

The true deer hunter was a melting pot of dreamer, weatherman, magician, student, artist, teacher and an ambassador for his calling. He was a dreamer because he was always dreaming about doing the impossible—matching wits with a mature buck and winning the contest! He was a weatherman out of necessity because he had to learn to read changing weather patterns like he read deer sign. Weather and timing sometimes had everything to do with success or failure.

A true deer hunter of yesteryear was a magician by design because he was always trying to pull a rabbit out of a hat. Sometimes he did just that! He was constantly learning new things to add to his arsenal of knowledge. At times, his skill level was so advanced and so second-nature that he became an artist in motion—i.e., the way he calmly made that impossible shot at a running deer with a rifle.

Much of his acquired knowledge was willingly and freely passed on to others whenever the opportunity presented itself because he genuinely wanted others to be able to share in and enjoy a rich American tradition the way he did. In so doing, he became a goodwill ambassador for one of our country's most cherished pastimes.

A deer hunter of yore was a man of great patience and great faith. If he was to succeed, he had to have faith in his creator and in his own ability. And let's don't forget that he was often a glutton for punishment. Rain, snow, sleet or hail, freezing temperatures, biting cold, wind, insects, cramped positions for long hours—you name it and he probably experienced it at one time or another during the season. The mythical mailman of generations past who delivered the mail in any kind of weather probably got his inspiration from whitetail hunters. In fact, he was probably a deer hunter himself.

The true deer hunter of the colorful past was a dedicated sportsman who lived by a set of inner rules and deep convictions that could not be compromised. Using the knowledge he had acquired every day to ply his trade, each new season became more exciting and more meaningful than the last. A thousand campfires ago, the true deer hunter of yesteryear lived for one more sunrise on opening day.

SOMEWHERE IN THE HARZ MOUNTAINS, GERMANY
We know our courageous GIs who stormed across France and Germany in 1944 and '45 fighting for freedom sorely missed baseball, apple pie and opening day of deer season back home, but don't fret—they certainly knew how to improvise in a pinch. These soldiers are securing an elegant young roe deer buck, probably taken with a trusty M-1, to their M8 armored car. It may be a cold snowy day in northern Germany, but these hearty soldiers will be feasting on venison and thinking of home tonight. Photo circa late 1944.

BUCKS PILED HIGH

At least 15 deer including several nice bucks are piled behind this group of hunters, indicating they've been doing quite a bit of shooting over the past few days. The pride of their accomplishment is written all over their faces. The photo is probably from the Upper Midwest, circa 1920.

OTT WENT DEER HUNTING

Ott and Lottie Buttemeirer stand in front of a magnificent buck resting in the trunk of their late 1940s Chevrolet. The back of the photo carries the inscription: "Been deer hunting." Apparently Ott had one whale of a day. Photo circa 1950.

Weaver Scope ad

CROSSBOW PRACTICE
This Arkansas crossbow hunter practices on a running deer target with his wooden crossbow. Used in both hunting and war over many centuries, crossbows have been around since ancient times. In more modern times, some adventurous sportsmen hunted deer with crossbows on a limited basis in the mid to late 1950s, but many of the bows of that vintage had limited range and were less than dependable in the field. Photo circa late 1950s.

BRINGING HOME THE BACON
The large tire wells on a 1946 Hudson four-door were tailor made for transporting deer. This well-dressed hunter shows off a fine 9-pointer. Photo circa late 1940s.

A CABIN IN THE WOODS
A sturdy cabin with an old moose skull over the doorway highlights a scene that has been acted out many thousands of times before in whitetail camps across the country. Two guides show off the deer they have helped procure as their well-dressed paying customers, or "sports," pose in front of cabin. The guide on the right appears to be holding a lever-action Winchester. Many of the guides who served in the Adirondacks and northern Maine in the late 1800s and early 1900s were full- or part-blooded Indians who had grown up living off the land. Photo circa early 1900s.

A THOUSAND CAMPFIRES AGO **187**

ELVIN SEES AND FRIENDS
Hunting with the Janvier Deer Club near Tuckertown, New Jersey during the 1935 shotgun season, Elvin W. Sees (center) shot this handsome eight-pointer. His was the best buck of the day. Photo courtesy of Elvin's great-grandson Jason M. Sterser.

BIG DEER FOR A BIG MAN
Stacey Jess of Glassboro, New Jersey killed this wide-spreading buck with a shotgun near Batson in 1934. Stacey obviously had no trouble man-handling the brute out of the woods. Photo courtesy of Joseph Rieger. The old photo hangs in Joseph's New Jersey hunting club.

NEW YORK GANG

The bucks are mostly yearlings, but the happy members of this sizable hunting club in Lava, New York near the Delaware River about 50 miles northwest of New York City have plenty of venison to go around. Photo taken November 1956.

SPOILS OF THE HUNT

As another hunting adventure draws to an end in the North Country, it's time to get your buck ready for shipping by rail to your home. Leaving deer camp is never easy, but the vivid memories help sustain the dedicated hunter until next time. Photo circa 1920.

BUCK POLE MEMORIES

With five deer hanging including three nice bucks, the hunters who have set up camp in this snow-covered section of woods must be having the time of their lives. There is nothing quite like the musky scent of several big bucks hanging in camp. The smokestack coming out of the large wall-tent in the background indicates the hunters inside will remain cozy and happy. Although this photo was taken about 85 years ago, it could easily be an American scene from last year. Photo circa 1930s.

MARLIN MEMORIES

These two Marlin men are obviously happy with the results of their hunt. Two young bucks rest on the fender of the late 1940s Chevrolet Fleetmaster Coupe, each taken with a Marlin 336. The man on the right has a Marlin 336 EE series carbine, while his companion on the right has a sleek 336a rifle with a half magazine. Introduced in 1948 by Marlin, the Model 336 rifle and carbine was offered in a number of calibers, the most popular being in .30-30 Winchester and .35 Remington. The Model 336 was a modern version of the popular Model 1893, produced from 1893 to 1936. What do you want to bet that one or both of these rifles are .30-30s? Note the custom luggage rack on top of the Chevy, probably made to hold camping gear. The license tag appears to be from Pennsylvania. Photo circa 1950.

BELKNAP HARDWARE & MANUFACTURING CO.

RIFLES
WINCHESTER HIGH POWER REPEATER

**Model 70 Super Grade. Bolt Action.
Staggered Box Type Magazine. 5 Shot.**

Barrel—24 inch tapered Winchester proof-steel. Bored, rifled and chambered.

Stock—Special design pistol grip stock of American walnut with check piece. Pistol grip cap. Grip and fore-end fancy checkered. Length pull 13½ inches; drop at comb 1 ⅝ inches; at heel 2 ⅝ inches. Steel butt plate.

Action—Bolt of up-turn, pull back mauser type.

Safety—Three position. On safe, both firing pin and bolt fully locked.

Sights—Redfield full gold bead front on forged ramp with removable sight cover. Winchester 22G open sporting rear sight.

Magazine—Staggered box type. Holds 5 cartridges.

Equipment—1 inch army type leather sling strap with quick detachable swivels.

Weight—About 8¼ lbs.

Length overall 44½ inches.

Each

No. D67-G7053C—Caliber 270 Winchester.. M$403 65 *$179 45*

No. D67-G7054C—Caliber 30-06 Springfield M 403 65 *179 45*

One in cardboard box; five in wood case; wt case 47½ lbs.

WINCHESTER, HIGH POWER REPEATER
Model 70, Bolt Action. 6 Shot, Clip Magazine.

Stock—Pistol grip N. R. A. type stock of walnut with full well shaped fore-end.

Barrel—Round, tapered, with ramp front sight base.

Sights—Front, Lyman gold bead with ⁵⁄₆₄ inch bead, mounted on ramp and furnished with sight cover. Rear, Winchester 22G open sporting.

Magazine—Holds 5 cartridges which with one in chamber makes 6 shots.

Safety—New Winchester design operating in horizontal plane and so not interfering with low mounted telescope sight. Quickly operated with tip of thumb providing fastest release available.

Weight—7¾ pounds. Each

No. D67-G7004C—30/06 caliber............M$272 10*$120 95*
No. D67-G7003C—270 Winchester caliber... M 272 10 *120 95*
No. D67-G7006C—257 Roberts caliber...... M 272 10 *120 95*
No. D67-G7008C—220 Winchester swift caliber M 272 10 *120 95*
No. D67-G7001C—22 Winchester Hornet caliber M 272 10 *120 95*
No. D67-G7060C—308 Caliber............M 272 10 *120 95*

One in cardboard box; five in case; wt case 40 lbs.

RIFLES
WINCHESTER, CENTER FIRE REPEATING
Model 70, Bolt Action, Monte Carlo Stock.

Stock—High comb Monte Carlo pistol grip sporting type of American walnut. Full, well shaped fore-end and grip checkered. Length 13 ⅝ inches.

Barrel—Round tapered, Winchester proof-steel.

Sights—Bead front on ramp base with removable sight cover. Folding leaf rear sight on all calibers. All model 70 receivers drilled and tapered for Lyman 48WJS, Redfield 70WT or 70WH, Vover 35M2, Williams foolproof and other micrometer receiver sight.

Magazine—Staggered box type with hinged floorplate. Holds five cartridges except 300 and 375 H & H Magnum, 4.

Safety—Three-position on safe, both firing pin and bolt fully locked. Intermediate position locks firing pin but not bolt.

Action—Upturn, pullback type bolt cocks on opening lift. Instantly removable. Famous Winchester speed lock.

Each

No. D67-G7033CN—270 Winchester Caliber;
24 inch barrel........................M$272 10*$120 95*

No. D67-G7034CN—30-06 Springfield Caliber;
24 inch barrel........................M 272 10 *120 95*

No. D67-G7036CN—257 Roberts Caliber; 24
inch barrel..........................M 272 10 *120 95*

No. D67-G7037CN—375 H&H Magnum; 25
inch barrel..........................M 272 10 *120 95*

No. D67-G7038CN—220 Swift Caliber; 26
inch barrel..........................M 272 10 *120 95*

No. D67-G7039CN—300 H&H Magnum; 26
inch barrel..........................M 272 10 *120 95*

One in cardboard box; wt each approx 8¼ lbs.

WINCHESTER REPEATER
348 CALIBER

**Standard Model No. 71, Lever Action. Solid
Frame. Tubular Magazine. 5 Shot.**

Barrel—24 inch round tapered with integral front ramp sight base. End of muzzle polished.

Stock—American walnut, sporting type, pistol grip with rubber cap. Semi-beavertail fore-end. Stock and fore-end checkered. Checkered steel shot gun butt plate. Length pull 13³⁄₁₆ inches; drop at comb 1¹³⁄₁₆ inches; drop at heel 2 inches.

Sling Strap—One inch leather sling strap attached by quick detachable swivels.

Sights—Lyman No. 13W on ramp base with detachable sight cover. Rear sight slot filled with blank. Winchester No. 98A peep sight mounted on the rear portion of the bolt.

Magazine—Holds four cartridges which with one in the chamber, makes rifle a five shot magazine.

Length—42¼ inches. Weight 8 lbs. Each

No. D67-G7101C—Chambered for super speed
348 Winchester center fire cartridges.....M$276 75*$123 00*

One in cardboard box; five in case; wt case 45 lbs.

This Winchester rifle ad is from a mid-1950s Belknap Hardware catalogue. Belknap Hardware & Manufacturing Co. was a highly successful manufacturing and retail mail order business based in Louisville, KY. William Burke Belknap started the company on the banks of the Ohio River in 1840. By the mid 20th century, the popular catalog featured over 3,500 pages and contained some 75,000 items. Each item was featured with hand drawn illustrations. Blue Grass baseball bats and a line of industrial crayons were among several of the company's brand labels along with many other hardware products. Sadly, the company went out of business in 1986 after over 140 years of continuous operation. Catalog /Winchester ad circa 1950s.

THE MEMORY OF OLD THREE LEGS LIVES ON

In 1945, a budding young Minnesota wildlife artist and avid deer hunter named Les Kouba (1917-1998) was sitting around the campfire with friends when he heard the story about the legend of Old Three Legs for the first time. He was so intrigued with the legend that he vowed to someday paint a picture of the rogue wolf.

Some 40 years later, in the mid-1980s, Kouba brought the legend to life with his historic painting of the three-legged wolf (see page 87). By then he had gained much recognition as a nationally acclaimed wildlife artist. Said to be the Norman Rockwell of Minnesota wildlife art, Kouba is best known for his amazing prints of waterfowl and pheasants, most of which depict 13 birds .

Throughout his long career, Kouba raised millions of dollars for wildlife and conservation efforts. He won the Federal Duck Stamp contest in 1958 and 1967 and was named Ducks Unlimited Artist of the year in 1976 and 1977. For years he operated American Wildlife Art Galleries in Minneapolis.

KOUBA'S HUNTING PARTY

Les Kouba had been a deer hunter for as long as he could remember. This photo was taken after the first day's successful hunt, northeast of Pine River, Minnesota, in 1945. Left to right: (back row) Les Kouba, "Swede" Tollefsrud, Oscar Thiers, Le Fitzgerald, Al Arones; (front row) Bo Berg and "Shorty" Tellefsrud.

Group photo of Les Kouba's 194 hunting party taken from bookle Kouba wrote to accompany his limite edition painting. Courtesy of Becke County Museum. The photo shows th deer hunting party that witnessed th story told by Oscar Thiers (front lef sitting) the evening before the openin of the 1945 deer hunting season. was that story—that night—that mad me decide that I would some da leave this story in "painting" form fo everyone to know and enjoy. Forty-fou years later it became a reality—the c painting *Old Three Legs*.

OLD THREE LEGS

Old Three Legs' eight-year war on sheep, turkeys, chickens and other livestock in northern Minnesota ended abruptly on Nov. 20, 1926 when Fred Darkow (second from left next to Old Three Legs) shot the legendary wolf while deer hunting with friends. The hunting party included (left to right) Jack Robbins, Darkow, Harry LaDue and George McCarthy (owner of the store behind him). Darkow was known as an accomplished deer hunter and crack shot. He was hunting with a Winchester Model 55 Standard lever-action repeater with a tang sight. Winchester introduced the Model 55 in June 1924, so Darkow's rifle must have been fairly new in 1926 when he downed Old Three Legs. The rifle came in two calibers; .30-30 and .32 Winchester Special. Darkow's rifle is believed to be a .30-30. Darkow died in 1987. Note: Today the mounted wolf and the rifle that brought him down are on display in the Becker County Museum in Detroit Lakes, Minnesota. Photo courtesy of Becker County Museum.

Winchester Model 55 belonging to Fred Darkow. Photo courtesy of Becker County Museum.

"In the breast of almost every meat hunter there beats the heart of a secret, frustrated trophy hunter. Few men, however addicted to venison, will pass up an antlered buck for the better-eating doe standing beside him. And fewer still, having shot an exceptional buck, will leave the great rack in the woods and pack out only the meat."

John Wootters
Hunting Trophy Deer (1977)

NON-TYPICAL MYSTERY BUCK

This massive drop-tined buck has a striking resemblance to the acclaimed "Hole in the Horn Buck" found dead beside a railroad track near Windham, Ohio around 1940 (although the Hole-in-the-Horn buck is considerably larger.) Several non-typical bucks with drop tines were taken in Ohio during the past few decades. We don't know where this photo was taken, and we don't know what became of the antlers, but the deer is certainly a one-of-a-kind, record-book animal. Armed with lever-action Winchesters (at least several original 1873s), these men seem to know they have achieved something quite out of the ordinary. Photo circa 1890.

The famed Hole in the Horn buck was found dead near a railroad track in Windham, Ohio in the early 1940s. A photo of the original mount appeared in the 1945 Edition of the Modern Taxidermy Directory (below).

The Missouri Monarch rack before it was mounted.

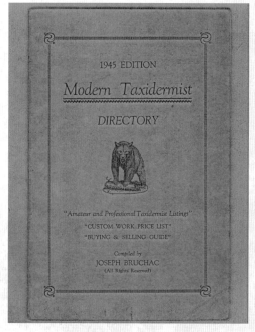

CHAPTER 14

BRAGGING RIGHTS

A century ago, most deer hunters were content to enjoy the camaraderie of deer camp for a week or so and go home with a supply of meat from the bucks or does taken on that hunt. Very little emphasis was placed on large antlers. Occasionally, a buck carrying an exceptional set of antlers would fall to some lucky hunter. Much celebration would take place in camp as the story was told over and over again around the fire, and that lucky hunter's esteem would go up considerably.

Most deer camps also seemed to have at least one legendary "ghost" buck with a mammoth set of antlers that was seen fleetingly from time to time. This fabled buck usually had a nickname like "Moses" or "Old Blue" or "the Swamp Ghost." He supposedly had dodged so much lead over time that he was deemed "charmed" and protected by some abnormal power. Each season his legend grew in stature.

Trophy racks might come from anywhere at the most unexpected times. While few hunters of yesteryear had the desire or the money to have their trophies mounted by a taxidermist, some definitely found a way to preserve their deer for posterity. Some simply mounted the antlers on a plaque instead of cutting them up for knife handles.

Whether killed by sheer accident by some kindred soul out trying to collect some winter venison, or by direct intent on the part of the hunter, legendary whitetail bucks usually came with exciting stories and plenty of "bragging rights."

THE HOLE IN THE HORN BUCK – ALMOST A WORLD RECORD

Considered by many to be the greatest whitetail of all time, the legendary "Hole in the Horn Buck" was found dead along the Erie Railroad near Windham, Ohio around 1940. One of the palmated drop tines on the right side of the rack had what appeared to be a small, clean bullet hole going through it about the size of a .22 slug. Later on, the huge trophy later became known as the Hole in the Horn Buck. The one-of-a-kind rack contained more than 60 points and had a spread of 35 inches. Most people assumed the deer had been killed by a train.

The trophy rack was later mounted by Ben H. Morgan, a taxidermist in Akron, Ohio. Reportedly one of the engineers on the train ended up with the incredible antlers and sold them for $25 to a local sportsman's club, known as the Kent Canadian Club to hang in the clubhouse/bar in Kent, Ohio. The rack hung in the clubhouse for more than 40 years and remained in relative obscurity. In 1983, antler collector Dick Idol bought the rack from the club and it soon received national exposure. The antlers were officially measured by Phil Wright, who at that time served as records chairman for the Boone and Crockett Club. Wright's entry score for the deer was 342 3/8 non-typical points. This should have been more than enough to make the deer a new world record but a new and unexpected

twist entered the picture.

Shortly before the Hole in the Horn Buck was measured in the summer of 1983, another giant non-typical buck had been found dead in St Louis County near the city of St. Louis. Known as the Missouri Monarch, this buck was later panel scored at B&C's 18th Awards Program in the summer of 1983. With a score of 333 7/8 non-typical points, it became a new world record. According to B&C's scoring procedure, the Hole in the Horn Buck was not eligible to be panel-measured until the next Awards Period in the summer of 1986. When that date arrived, the Hole in the Horn Buck was panel scored at 328 2/8 points, a little over five points less than the Missouri Monarch.

The Missouri Monarch (above) stood as the ranking world record while the now world-famous Hole in the Horn Buck ranked No. 2. Even though the Hole in the Horn Buck is considerably larger than the huge "mystery" buck taken back around 1890, there are similarities in the two racks. Wouldn't it be something if that buck had come from northeastern Ohio.

THE REST OF THE STORY:
THE BUCK ASHE SHEDS

Volume 1 of *Dawn of American Deer Hunting* featured a story about the greatest buck ever taken in the southeastern U.S.—the Buck Ashe trophy killed in Monroe County, Georgia in November 1961. Scoring 191⅛ typical points, it became the Georgia state record typical whitetail.

Ashe's story was amazing in itself. A dedicated bow hunter, he killed the deer with a rifle and always regretted it. It was never scored at the time it was killed, and Ashe eventually moved to Tulsa, Oklahoma. In 1999, after the rack was located and returned to Georgia where it was officially measured, an even more bizarre story unfolded involving the deer's shed antlers.

In the spring of 1961, both shed antlers from the Buck Ashe trophy were picked up in Monroe County by different individuals nearly a mile apart. Because of the sheer size of the antlers, they were highly treasured by their owners.

A Bizarre Coincidence

In March 1961, 26-year-old Damus Mullinax of Chamblee, Georgia was out "rambling in the woods" in Monroe County where he frequently hunted about a mile from the spot where a youngster named Gordon McMullen had found another huge shed two months earlier. Mullinax stumbled upon the left shed antler from an enormous buck that carried five typical points. The tip of the brow tine and the tip of the G-3 had been gnawed off by rodents. The main beam measured 30⅛ inches in length while the G-2 measured 14⅝ inches. The left shed scored 92⅝ inches.

Thirty-eight years later in February 1999, a friend of Mullinax's son, Denver, saw an article in *Whitetail* magazine. That friend called Denver and told him about the Buck Ashe Trophy. Coincidentally, Denver knew Buck's son, Mark, who lived in North Georgia. Denver called Mark and told him he thought he had the left shed antler from Buck's trophy deer.

Gordon McMullen holds both shed antlers.

The Buck Ashe shed antlers compared to a smaller antler.

Almost Destroyed by a House Fire

In mid-February 1961, 14-year-old Gordon McMullen of Forsyth, Georgia was rabbit hunting with his two brothers when he found a massive right-side shed antler in a pine thicket. It contained five typical points and several burr points.

The antler was picked up in the general vicinity where Buck Ashe would later shoot his record whitetail the following November. The estimated six-inch brow tine had been broken off. The main beam measured nearly 30 inches and the G-2 tine measured nearly 15 inches in length. The base of the antler contained four short burr points (very similar to those on the deer Buck Ashe would later shoot). The antler measured 85⅝ inches without the brow tine.

McMullen treasured the antler and always wondered what had become of the deer that had carried it.

In 1994, 33 years after finding the antler, McMullen and his wife were in a Forsyth, Georgia restaurant eating lunch when someone rushed in and told them their house was on fire. They quickly rushed to the scene and saw their two-story house engulfed in flames. At McMullen's request, a fireman ran into the burning downstairs den and salvaged the cherished antler that was resting on the fireplace. The base was already charred from the intense heat and flames.

Five years later, in February 1999, I wrote a story in *North American Whitetail* magazine about the recently discovered Buck Ashe trophy from Georgia. After the story was out, a short account ran in a local newspaper in Forsyth. McMullen's brother Mike saw the article, and told Gordon, "I think we've finally found your buck."

Buck Ashe was a passionate deer hunter who dedicated the best years of his life to hunting, fishing and pursuing other outdoor interests. He passed away in 2017.

Buck Ashe (left) and his good friend Olin Hunter (right) who insisted Buck go hunting that day in November 1961 and loaned him a Marlin .30-30.

United After 38 Years

When both shed antlers were finally reunited in 1999, there was no question they had been the previous years' antlers from the Buck Ashe trophy. The Buck Ashe trophy gross-scored 210⅝ inches. With 18⅝ inches in deductions from six abnormal points, it netted 191⅝. Amazingly, the shed antlers from the year before would have scored considerably higher than Ashe's trophy deer because the tines are longer and the deductions for abnormal points would have been less than 10 inches. Giving the sheds the same 22⅜ inch inside spread as the trophy antlers and a 6¼-inch right brow tine (matching the left side), the shed antlers from the year before might have netted 200 inches or better.

THE IVAN MASCHER BUCK
MAKING BOWHUNTING HISTORY IN NEBRASKA

Ivan Mascher, holding his old Bear recurve, with his Nebraska megabuck. Above: Mascher poses with his giant buck shortly after he arrowed it in 1961.

Avid bow-hunter Ivan Mascher of Sidney, Nebraska, made bowhunting history of sorts on Nov. 27, 1961 when he arrowed a massive, 16-point non-typical giant near the town of Valley (just west of Omaha) that tallied 198 points. At the time, Ivan made his home on three acres of rented farmland on the outskirts of Omaha. During the late 1950s, when he was in his 20s, he became very interested in bowhunting.

"We were as poor as church mice back then, and my wife and I were trying to raise three kids on about $65 a week," Ivan remembered. "But I bit the bullet and bought myself a 45-pound Bear Grizzly recurve bow from a friend who sold archery equipment. I also got some of his handmade wooden shafts tipped with Bear broadheads."

If you've ever stared eye-to-eye at a trophy whitetail at close range while trying to come to full draw and place an arrow into an area the size of a small saucer, you know how difficult that feat can be. But try doing it with a primitive recurve bow and no sights like Ivan Mascher did nearly 57 years ago.

"I was hunting near a large sumac patch that day and all of a sudden I started hearing a terrific noise in there, like someone beating on trees with a big stick."

Suddenly, a giant buck appeared, and instinct took over. Ivan made a perfect broadside shot at about 20 yards. At the time he shot his great buck, Ivan was in contention for having both a state record by bow as well as a potential archery world record. But Fate had other plans.

One season later in 1962 Del Austin arrowed an incredible 279⅞-inch behemoth out in Hall Co. (a little over 100 miles west of Omaha). By the end of the Boone and Crockett Awards Period in 1963, Ivan's buck was edged out by Del's world-class megabuck. Today, Ivan's awesome trophy hangs in Cabela's Sydney, Nebraska store for all the world to admire.

BRAGGING RIGHTS

JERSEY'S FINEST
THE NORMAN TAYLOR BUCK
NEW JERSEY STATE RECORD NON-TYPICAL

This massive, wide-racked whitetail resembles a mule deer in many ways. It was brought down by Norman Taylor near New Lisbon, New Jersey in November 1946. Hunting in Burlington County with the Earlin Gun Club of Browns Mill near the Fort Dix Army base, Taylor shot the 31-point giant with a shotgun while participating in a deer drive. Deer drives involving numerous club members were a common method of hunting in those days.

The huge rack, scored for the first time in the mid-1980s, netted 214⅜ non-typical B&C points. The 31-point giant reportedly dressed out at 179 pounds.

Not only is the Taylor buck the largest non-typical ever taken in New Jersey, it's also the largest whitetail ever taken by a shotgun in that state. The Earlin Gun Club of Browns Mill is still in existence today.

Special thanks to Nelson and Dawn Roque of New Jersey Big Bucks for providing photos.

The original old mount of the Norman Taylor buck.

Hunter Norman Taylor (left) and his friend Joe Anderson (right) pose with the wide-spreading buck shortly after it was taken on a New Jersey deer drive in 1946.

THE BILL ARRE BUCK
NO. 2 SHOTGUN BUCK IN NEW JERSEY

Much like Norman Taylor, New Jersey shotgun hunter Bill Arre was also participating in a deer drive back in the day when he encountered an extraordinary buck. Arre was a member of the Pleasant Plains Gunning Club (also still in existence). He was hunting on club land with a group near Tom's River in Ocean County in November 1959.

As one of the designated drivers, Arre reportedly spotted a large buck lying close to the ground in an attempt to remain hidden and allow him to pass by, a ploy often successfully used by crafty bucks during drives.

Not to be outmaneuvered, Arre wasted little time in shooting the big buck with a load of buckshot. The recently measured, 20-point trophy rack gross-scored 201 4/8 non-typical points and netted 193 4/8. The estimated field-dressed weight of the huge buck was between 170 and 180 pounds.

The Bill Arre trophy now stands as New Jersey's No. 2 shotgun buck of all time. Special thanks to Nelson and Dawn Roque of New Jersey Big Bucks for providing photos.

New mount of the Bill Arre buck.

Note: Shooting a buck in its bed was perfectly legal in 1959, although it does bring up an ethical question in which there are pros and cons on both sides of the issue. Although it is considered highly unsportsmanlike by most hunters in today's world, who's to say what went through Bill Arre's mind in the split second he had to make the decision.

The old axion, 'if you can hang a ring on it, it's a point," apparently credited the Bill Arre buck with a number of extra tines over the years. In truth, the rack had only 20 scoreable points when it was officially measured.

Old mount of the Bill Arre buck. The rack grossed 201 4/8 non-typical points.

BRAGGING RIGHTS

NORTH DAKOTA WHITETAIL GEM
ROGER RITCHIE'S MIDWEST MONSTER

Fifty years ago, Roger Ritchie shot a massive, 31-point non-typical buck near Stanley, North Dakota. Being from Maryland, Ritchie had been stationed at Minot Air Force base in Stanley. The world-class whitetail instantly became a state record, but after Ritchie returned home, the trophy drifted into obscurity.

Ritchie was originally from Old Town, Maryland. Born in 1946, he joined the Air Force in the late '60s. After his discharge in May 1967, he apparently lived in Stanley for several years before returning home. An avid outdoorsman, one of the reasons he stayed in the area might have been the incredible hunting and fishing opportunities.

On Nov. 16, 1968, Ritchie was hunting in Lostwood National Wildlife Refuge north of Stanley with a friend named Dave Gonzales when he crossed paths with one of the greatest whitetails to ever grace the high plains of North Dakota.

According to a short newspaper account written about Ritchie's achievement, it took three shots to bring down the extraordinary buck. The deer had 31 measurable points and reportedly weighed 187 pounds field dressed.

Ritchie's buck was entered in the all-time B&C record book, but a math error was made in the score sheet and the entry score was listed as 248⅝ (instead of the actual score of 254⅝). The six-point deficit was still good enough to make Ritchie's awesome buck the No. 10 non-typical whitetail of all time. The math error was later discovered and the correct score of 254⅝ was listed in later editions of the record book.

Ritchie returned to his native Maryland a few years after killing the deer. He soon met

This photo of the mounted 31-point North Dakota trophy was probably taken several years after Ritchie shot the huge buck. Ritchie's scoped Winchester Model 70 bolt-action rifle and all four hooves from the state record whitetail bare testimony to the high regard the young hunter had for his once-in-a-lifetime trophy.

Appearing in the *Minot Daily News* on Nov. 22, 1968, this is the only-known photo taken of Roger Ritchie posed with his great Stanley County, 31-point buck.

At the time it was killed in 1968, Roger Ritchie's colossal North Dakota giant ranked as the 10th largest non-typical whitetail ever taken by a hunter.

the girl of his dreams and the couple married in early 1973. Two months later, on March 9, Ritchie was killed in a motorcycle accident. He was 27.

"Roger was always an avid hunter," his wife Debbie stated years later. "He hunted all the time. He wanted to own his own gun shop. He was going to business school at the time he was killed. He was working for W.D. Grant's Department Store in Cumberland, Maryland in 1972 and the early months of 1973. His deer head hung in that store for a while and it always drew plenty of attention."

Despite his short life, Roger Ritchie's legacy to the hunting world is the great whitetail buck he shot on the North Dakota plains on a cold November day in 1968. Today, the trophy head hangs proudly in the Wonders of Wildlife Museum at Bass Pro Shop in Springfield, Missouri.

SONNY'S MOUNTAIN MONARCH
TENNESSEE'S GREATEST TYPICAL EVER

By the time he was 21 years old, Sonny Foster of Rockwood, Tennessee was a seasoned deer hunter. Hunting whitetails was a much anticipated family tradition. On the second day of the 1959 season, Sonny was out with his father and a group of close friends.

"In those days, you needed a four-wheel drive to get back to the remote places we liked to hunt," Sonny remembered. "My father-in-law owned a 1947 Willys Jeep. It was probably the only four-wheel drive vehicle within 100 miles. Many a cold morning six or eight of us would pile into that thing in the freezing darkness and head back 10 or 12 miles into the mountains. We spent a lot of time scouting in places no one else would go, and the buck sign we found was unbelievable."

The Fosters were hunting in a remote area just south of what is now Catoosa Wildlife Management Area. Opening day had been a disappointment for Sonny and his gang. But now, despite the bitter cold on the second day, Sonny was anxious to get back in an area where some sign from a large buck had been found. Little could he imagine that he was about to encounter the largest buck ever seen in the state of Tennessee.

"It all happened pretty fast," Sonny remembered. "About 30 minutes after daylight, Jackie Byrd, a friend who was hunting with us that day, fired three shots down the ridge from where I was standing. A few seconds later, a large-bodied buck with the biggest set of horns I'd ever seen came running by me."

Sonny instinctively drew a bead with his Model 94 Winchester .30-30 and fired at the running deer. The huge buck collapsed in a heap. As Sonny approached the downed giant,

At the time it was killed in 1959, Sonny Foster's incredible Tennessee mountain buck ranked No. 6 in the all-time B&C record book. At 186 1/8 typical points, it also became a Tennessee state record. It has remained as Tennessee's best typical buck for 59 years.

A 70s-something Sonny Foster shows off his buck in 2006, while a somewhat younger Sonny Foster (below) displays the old mountain warrior in a mid-1980s photo. Sadly, Foster passed away several years ago.

the deer suddenly jumped up and tried to run off. Sonny fired two more shots. His second shot hit the buck in the neck, putting him down for good.

"Even though he had a huge set of antlers, people thought more about his body size than his horns," Sonny remembered.

The buck weighed about 230 pounds field dressed. Since the deer had a wide-spreading rack equal to its weight in every respect, Sonny was bent on having his trophy mounted. While at the taxidermist, a state biologist measured the antlers for the record book. Incredibly, Sonny's 11-point mountain monarch scored 186⅛ typical points. This was only 20 points less than the ranking world record and Sonny's buck stood as the No. 6 typical whitetail in the all-time Boone and Crockett Record Book.

Although records for big deer did not exist in Tennessee in 1959, Sonny's trophy eventually was declared a state record, a position it still holds to this day.

BRAGGING RIGHTS **205**

"I don't know a hunting achievement quite equal to outguessing an old whitetail."

Archibald Rutledge
Those Were the Days (1955)

JOE FRAZER WITH HIS ICONIC WILLYS JEEP

Joe Frazer (1892-1971), president of the Willys-Overland Company, puts what appears to be a venison ham into his 1940s-vintage Jeep. His companion appears to be some type of retriever, possibly a Portuguese water dog. Having had a long association with the auto industry, Frazer took over as president of the ailing Willys-Overland Company in 1939. After the war broke out in 1941, he was credited with almost single-handedly selling the "Jeep" concept to the Army as an off-road scouting and reconnaissance vehicle. Sharing the heavy manufacturing load with Ford and Bantam, the Willys-Overland MB (Jeep) became the most versatile World War II vehicle the military had ever seen. General Dwight D. Eisenhower reportedly claimed, "America could not have won World War II without it." In the late 1940s and early '50s, Willys-Overland began to manufacture the Jeep for the general public. It quickly became as much of a success with hunters and outdoorsmen for off-road travel as it had been with the military. Today, some 70 years later, the Jeep brand is still as popular as ever. Photo circa 1942.

CHAPTER 15

LEGENDS OF THE HUNT:
MEN AND WOMEN WHO MADE THEIR MARK

PAPA FRED BEAR IN HIS ELEMENT
"Papa" Fred Bear poses with a wide-spreading Michigan buck. Fred traveled the globe in pursuit of many of the most sought-after big game trophies but, deep in his heart, he always held a special place for his beloved Michigan whitetails.

It seems that every generation of deer hunters produces its own crop of men who become hunting legends. Some of our earliest deer hunting legends came to us through the works of great writers like James Fenimore Cooper with his iconic character Natty Bumpo, the "Deerslayer." A real life hunting hero like Davy Crockett may be best known for his bear hunting escapades, but he grew up hunting Tennessee whitetails. The same is true with legendary pathfinder Daniel Boone. He survived many a wilderness adventure on deer meat. In fact, during his many years as a market hunter, he killed literally hundreds of whitetails for their meat and skins.

Nearly all of the great hunters who made a name for themselves in the early 1800s cut their teeth on America's most revered big game animal. The following stories highlight some of our most enduring American deer hunters.

CUSTER THE HUNTER
LIFE ON THE PLAINS

Custer killed this bull elk during the Yellowstone Expedition in the summer of 1873 with an 1871 Remington rolling block rifle. The expedition was organized by the US Army to explore the Dakota and Montana territories in order to survey a route for the Northern Pacific Railroad along the Yellowstone River. Custer killed several elk during that expedition, including, "a fine large buck-elk taller than Dandy (his horse) weighing, cleaned, 800 pounds, and with the handsomest antlers I ever saw." Remington Arms Company has a letter from Custer extolling the virtues of his rolling block rifle. Some say that he was carrying his faithful rolling block at the Little Big Horn three years later.

We mostly remember him as the hard-charging, flamboyant cavalry leader whose serious error in judgment cost him and his troops dearly on June 25, 1876 on a grassy hillside in eastern Montana. George Armstrong Custer (1840-1876) had greatly underestimated the size of the massive Cheyenne and Sioux village discovered by his scouts on the banks of the Little Big Horn River. And he greatly underestimated the Indians' will to stand and fight. In the past, the hostile Indians had always tried to run whenever the soldiers showed up near a village—always determined to protect the women and children first and get them out of harm's way. But not on this day.

On this historic day, led by their determined spiritual leader Sitting Bull, they would stand and fight. After splitting up his command so

Pen-and-Ink illustration of General Custer with his horse, Vic, and his stag hounds and deer hounds.

the village could be attacked from several sides (ensuring the Indians could not get away), Custer isolated his small command, and he and some 200 of his men were overrun and wiped out by 3,000 determined warriors.

Dozens of books have been written about Custer the soldier and the Battle of the Little Big Horn, but there is another side to the impulsive "Boy General" that has received little attention.

Custer was a passionate hunter throughout his short life. He loved guns and hunting dogs. He cut his teeth hunting whitetails in Michigan and Ohio where he grew up. He also hunted small game as a boy. He developed his lifelong love and appreciation for good dogs by shooting rabbits and birds and by spending many a moonlit night following the hounds and chasing 'coons.

Custer later became a prolific writer during the relatively short time he spent on the western plains, but he never wrote much about his early days hunting whitetails. Once he reached the plains, he graduated to bigger and much more exotic western game—elk, grizzlies, mule deer (called black-tail deer in the 1870s), antelope and buffalo. The whitetails of his youth were more or less forgotten. He never lived long enough to write about some of his early whitetail exploits. He was only 36 when he died.

During the Civil War, the Boy General had little time to hunt, but he did do some limited hunting whenever he went back home to Michigan on leave. After the war, he resumed his passion for hunting on the Kansas plains and beyond. Here, new horizons opened up with countless opportunities.

In the mid-1870s, the biggest prize of all for serious hunters like Custer from the East or Midwest was the iconic buffalo. Buffalo hunting reigned supreme.

To an eastern sportsman in the late 1870s and 1880s, making the difficult journey to the plains by rail and participating in a rip-roaring buffalo hunt on horseback where the quarry was often shot at close range with a pistol, was akin to a 20th century hunter going after one of the big five in Africa. It took almost as much travel and preparation and the danger factor was considerable.

For a high-energy, high-profile soldier like

Custer who had experienced life-threatening combat almost daily during the last year and a half of the Civil War, frontier life was monotonous, boring and at times almost unbearable. Encounters with Indians were rare, and Custer and many other cavalry officers spent much of their time hunting and fishing.

Custer usually rode the best thoroughbred horses money could buy, both for hunting and fighting Indians, and at the time of his death he owned one of the finest packs of hounds on the western plains.

Several years before his death, he became very successful at doing his own taxidermy work. He often worked long hours into the night preserving skins and mounting the heads of trophies he had killed. He even mounted a life-size elk and donated it to the Audubon Club in Detroit because he didn't have room for it in his quarters.

He once wrote his wife, Libby, "I have succeeded so well in taxidermy that I can take the head and neck of an antelope, fresh from the body, and in two hours have it fully ready for preservation."

Between 1867 and 1875, Custer wrote 15 articles or "letters," as he called them, for the New York based sportsman's journal, *Turf, Field and Farm* magazine. Using the pen name Nomad, his first letter about hunting appeared in the September 21, 1867 issue.

In that letter he described Kansas as a sportsman's paradise. Most of the wild game he brought in became table fare: "We had buffalo, elk, black-tail deer (mule deer), antelope, turkey, geese, duck, quail and several varieties of snipe."

Custer also mentioned experimenting with that much-fabled mountain-man "delicacy," broiled beaver tail, which he found to be full of gristle and disgusting. On the other hand, he found broiled rattlesnake meat to be "as white and as delicate as that of a young quail."

Custer poses with his first grizzly taken during the controversial Black Hills Expedition of 1874. It reportedly took several shots to bring down the big bear. Custer poses with Bloody Knife (on left, one of his favorite scouts), Captain William Ludlow, the chief engineer of the expedition (far right, who also shot the bear) and "Lonesome" Charley Reynolds in Buckskins (on right) who died at the Little Big Horn with Custer. Photographed by William Illingworth.

Close Call with a Buffalo

After the Civil War, Custer was stationed in Kentucky and West Texas for short stints, and he hunted whitetails in both places. But the moment he reached the plains of Kansas, he set his sights on killing his first buffalo. He got his chance while on a scouting trip near Walnut Creek. The experience almost ended in disaster. His hounds had struck the trail of an antelope, and he followed it a short distance. But not wanting to get too far from the main body of soldiers because there were hostile Indians in the area, he called the dogs in and headed back to rejoin the column.

Nearing the column, he spotted what he thought was a buffalo some two miles distant. He headed toward the animal at a slow pace since his horse was winded from running the

In 1872, Buffalo Bill Cody, shown here adorned in his Wild West Show attire, along with George Custer, hosted Grand Duke Alexei Alexandrovich Romanov of Russia on a highly publicized buffalo hunt in Nebraska. The hunt went well and Alexei killed several buffalo.

antelope. As he approached what turned out to be a lone bull, the buffalo saw him and the chase began.

After galloping some three miles, Custer finally drew up beside the animal. He drew his pistol "of the Savage pattern" and prepared to shoot the beast behind the shoulder. Just as he was aiming his pistol at the "fatal spot," the buffalo veered toward the horse, causing the horse to veer also, and Custer accidentally discharged the pistol, hitting his horse just behind the ears and killing it instantly.

The horse went end over end, and Custer was thrown 10 feet over its head. When he regained his senses, the buffalo was standing a few paces away, looking at him with a menacing stare. Fortunately, Custer was not hurt, and the buffalo went on his way.

Custer walked some two miles back toward the column and finally saw dust on the horizon where he was later reunited with his men.

That same afternoon, the column ran into another small herd of buffalo. Mounted on a new horse, Custer shot his first buffalo.

Over the next nine years, Custer did considerable buffalo hunting on the plains. In 1872, he and Buffalo Bill Cody served as "celebrity" hunting guides on one of the most publicized buffalo hunts in history, a "royal hunt" for Grand Duke Alexei Alexandrovich of Russia, the 22-year-old son of Czar Alexander II. The hunt took place on the Nebraska prairie where the young Grand Duke ended up killing two buffalo.

Had Custer lived beyond the age of 36, he certainly would have pursued his hunting and taxidermy passion and likely written a great deal more about his hunting exploits.

ANNIE OAKLEY
LITTLE MISS SURE SHOT

America's most beloved female sharpshooter was born Phoebe Ann Moses in west-central Ohio in August, 1860. Variations of the spelling of her name were Mosey, Mosie and Mauzy. Her father was known to be an avid hunter and sportsman. Sadly, he died of pneumonia when Annie was 6 years old. The family suffered great poverty and Annie's mother struggled to feed her children. Annie began to trap small animals like rabbits and quail to put food on the table. At age 8, she killed her first squirrel with her father's old muzzleloader, thus launching her career as a gifted rifle shooter. She later remembered the incident as a thrilling and life-changing experience.

Annie likely inherited her love of shooting and hunting from her father. After a miserable two years of being bound out as a domestic housemaid for an abusive family, Annie returned home and helped her mother and siblings by resuming her passion for hunting. She was so successful at killing an occasional deer and small game animals with her beloved father's old guns—mostly rabbits, quail and squirrels—that she began selling the meat to a local grocery store. The grocer in turn began selling the meat to hotels in Cincinnati and other nearby cities. Eventually, Annie earned enough money to pay off her mother's $200 mortgage.

Annie soon became very well known for her hunting abilities and amazing shooting skills. In 1875, when she was 15, the famous Baughman and Butler shooting act was being performed in Cincinnati (the exact date has been disputed and could have been

As a young girl, Annie Oakley honed her shooting skills by hunting small game and deer in her native Ohio woods.

as late as 1881.) Professional marksman Frank Butler (1847-1926), an Irish immigrant, placed a $100 bet with Cincinnati hotel owner Jack Frost claiming that he could out-shoot any local resident.

On Thanksgiving Day, Frost arranged a shooting match between Butler and young Annie, reportedly saying, "The last opponent Butler expected was a five-foot-tall, fifteen-year-old girl named Annie." No doubt Butler was quite surprised. After hitting 24 live birds in a row and missing the 25th, he lost both the match and the $100.

Undaunted and intrigued with the petite and beautiful young shooting expert, Butler began courting Annie, and the pair started performing shooting exhibitions together. Annie used the

Annie holds her much-loved Parker Brothers 12-gauge shotgun while next to her are two other favorites: a Stevens Model 31 Tip Up .22 rimfire with what appears to have a custom stock and trigger assembly, and a slide-action shotgun, possibly an 1890 Spencer-Bannerman. The Stevens Model 31 Tip Up was made from 1886 to 1916. The pistol in the foreground is probably a Stevens Tip Up .22. Photo circa early 1890s.

LEGENDS OF THE HUNT: MEN AND WOMEN WHO MADE THIER MARK

Annie Oakley shoots an apple off a dog's head with a .22 rifle at 30 feet. She performed this and many other shooting acts over her 16-year career with Buffalo Bill Cody's Wild West Show.

stage name, "Annie Oakley." They married some time later after Frank's divorce from a previous marriage was final. The couple never had children.

In 1885, Frank and Annie joined Buffalo Bill Cody's Wild West Show. She was an immediate sensation. Because of her petite five-foot stature and incredible shooting abilities, her soon-to-be special friend and fellow performer, Sioux medicine man and spiritual leader Chief Sitting Bull, crowned her with the Lakota nickname of "Watanya Cicilla" or "Little Sure Shot." Buffalo Bill always called her "Li'l Miss," and the lasting nickname of "Little Miss Sure Shot" soon evolved.

Frank and Annie stayed with the Wild West Show for 16 seasons. Annie earned top wages and she was quite generous with her money. She and Frank often donated money to orphanages and other children's charities. Annie also stood up for women and women's rights. She strongly believed that every woman in America should be proficient with a gun, and she reportedly taught more than 15,000 women how to shoot firearms during her lifetime.

When war with Spain seemed imminent, Annie wrote a letter to President William McKinley on April 5, 1898, "offering the government the services of a company of 50 lady sharpshooters who would provide their own arms and ammunition should the U.S. go to war with Spain." The offer was not accepted, but Theodore Roosevelt did name his volunteer cavalry unit the "Rough Riders" after "Buffalo Bill's Wild West and Congress of Rough Riders of the World," where Annie Oakley was a major star.

In 1901, the same year McKinley was fatally shot by an assassin, injuries from a train accident in Virginia caused Annie to retire from the grueling schedule of the Wild West Show. She and Frank lived out their retirement in Maryland and enjoyed many hunting trips in Florida and North Carolina.

Annie Oakley passed away in 1926 as a result of pernicious anemia, a blood disorder in which a lack of vitamin B-12 causes a shortage of red blood cells. Frank Butler, her husband and soul mate of some 50 years, refused to eat. He died 18 days later of a broken heart.

Annie holds one of her favorite rifles, a Winchester Model 1873 lever action, in this publicity show to promote Buffalo Bill's Wild West Show. Photo circa late 1880s.

Annie poses at a shooting exhibition in 1922 with a Winchester Model 1873 given to her by her dear friend Buffalo Bill Cody years earlier. A lifelong deer and big game hunter, Annie owned an 1892 Winchester with a whitetail buck engraved on it. She died four years after this photo was taken at age 62 from a blood disorder.

Annie performs a trick shot with a mirror. Photo 1890.

LEGENDS OF THE HUNT: MEN AND WOMEN WHO MADE THIER MARK

THEODORE ROOSEVELT
EXCERPTS FROM HUNTING TRIPS OF A RANCHMAN

Decked out in buckskins and moccasins he loved to wear when pursuing whitetails, Theodore Roosevelt holds his custom Winchester Model 1876 half-magazine, lever-action rifle in .45-75 caliber.

Without question, our 26th president was the greatest hunting president in history. Theodore Roosevelt was also one of the greatest conservationists this country has ever known. He was a dedicated student of nature and one of the driving forces behind the conservation movement that began in the early 1900s.

Aided by his alliterative "big stick," his vision for what needed to be done and his sheer force of will resulted in many vital conservation initiatives being passed into law.

Although Roosevelt's life only spanned 61 short years, he was a passionate, high energy individual who packed a lot of living into those years. In addition to being one of our most visionary presidents, he was an explorer, a war hero, a Nobel Prize winner, a Life member of the NRA, one of the founders of the Boone and Crockett Club and an avid world-class hunter. He was also a prolific writer who penned some 40 books and numerous articles in his lifetime. Many of those books are about his hunting exploits in North America and Africa.

In 1884, at age 26, Roosevelt lost his wife shortly after she had given birth to a daughter. The grief-stricken young man traveled west from his home in New York and lived on a ranch in the Dakota badlands for the next three years. Out of this experience came some of his greatest hunting literature, including several stories about chasing gnarly whitetails on his ranch in the Dakota river bottoms.

When you read excerpts from Roosevelt's writing, you'll find that not much has really changed in the 130 years since those magical words were written. Other than the camouflage we wear today and the modern high-tech weapons we use, Roosevelt's timeless words could have been written last season.

Roosevelt cut his hunting teeth on whitetails, and he always held a special place in his heart for America's most revered big game animal. But like other veteran big game hunters/writers who went on to chase bigger and more exotic species, he wrote very little about whitetails after he began to expand his hunting horizons. How fortunate we are to have some of his classic writings from those cherished cowboy days in North Dakota.

Always a skilled horseman, Theodore Roosevelt holds his trusty 1903 Springfield Armory .30-06 rifle, a veteran of many hunts. Photo circa 1910.

Following are some excerpts about how Roosevelt hunted his river bottom whitetails.

"White-tails are very canny, and know perfectly well what threatens danger and what does not. Their larger, and to my mind nobler, relation, the black-tail (mule deer), is if anything easier to approach and kill, and yet it is by no means so apt to stay in the immediate neighborhood of a ranch, where there is always more or less noise and confusion. The bottom on which my ranch-house stands is a couple of miles in length and well-wooded; all through last summer it was the home of a number of white-tails; and most of them are on it to this moment.

"Throughout the day the white-tail keeps in the densest thickets, choosing if possible those of considerable extent. For this reason they are confined to the bottoms of rivers and the mouths of the largest creeks, the cover elsewhere being too scanty to suit them. It is very difficult to make them leave one of their haunts during the daytime. They lie very close, permitting a man to pass right by them; and the twigs and branches surrounding them are so thick and interlaced that they can hear the approach of any one from a long distance off, and hence are rarely surprised.

"If they think there is danger that the intruder will discover them, they arise and skulk silently

LEGENDS OF THE HUNT: MEN AND WOMEN WHO MADE THIER MARK **217** off through the thickest part of the brush. If followed, they keep well ahead, moving perfectly noiselessly through the thicket, often going round in a circle and not breaking cover until hard pressed; yet all the time stepping with such sharp-eyed caution that the pursuing hunter will never get a glimpse of the quarry, though the patch of brush may not be fifty rods across.

"The best way to kill white-tail is to still-hunt carefully through their haunts at dusk, when the deer leave the deep recesses in which their day-beds lie, and come out to feed in the more open parts. For this kind of hunting, no dress is so good as buckskin suit and moccasins. The moccasins enable one to tread softly and noiselessly, while the buckskin suit is of a most inconspicuous color, and makes less rustling than any other material when passing among projecting twigs.

"Care must be taken to always hunt up wind, and to advance without any sudden motions, walking close to the edges of the thickets, and keeping a sharp look-out, as it is of the first importance to see the game before the game sees you. The feeding grounds of deer may vary. If they are on a bottom studded with dense copses, they move out on the open between them; if they are in a dense wood, they feed along its edges; but by preference, they keep in the little glades and among the bushes underneath the trees.

"If the deer is standing just out of a fair-sized wood, it can often be obtained by creeping up along the edge; if seen among the large trees, it is even more easily still-hunted, as a tree trunk can be readily kept in line with the quarry, and thus prevent its suspecting any approach. But

This room at Theodore Roosevelt's Sagamore Hill displayed several of his big game trophies. Built between 1884 and 1885, the 23-room mansion served as the summer white house for TR.

This engraved Winchester 1876 with a half-round octagonal barrel, pistol grip, and deluxe checkered wood was one of several Winchesters used by Roosevelt. The knife in his belt is a custom sterling silver Bowie made by Tiffany and Co., New York. Photo circa 1903.

tail. The head is carried low and well forward in running as the buck, when passing swiftly through thick underbrush, usually throws his horns back almost on his shoulders, with his nose held straight in front. Whitetail venison is, in season, most delicious eating, only inferior to the mutton of the mountain sheep."

Roosevelt owned at least two Winchester lever-action rifles during the time he spent on his ranch: a Model 1873 in .32-20 Winchester and a Model 1876 .45-75 Winchester. He probably used these rifles for whitetails. He also owned a Sharpes .45 caliber 1874 Sporting rifle and a 10-gauge double-barreled shotgun that he used on waterfowl.

During his first trip to the Dakota badlands in 1883, he wrote that he bagged "one bison and a black-tail buck" with the Sharps.

(From *Hunting Trips of a Ranchman*, published by G. P. Putnam's Sons, 1883.)

only a few white-tail are killed by regular and careful stalking; in much greater numbers of instances, the hunter simply beats patiently and noiselessly from leeward, carefully through the clumps of trees and bushes, always prepared to see his game and with his rifle at the ready.

"Sooner or later, as he steals round a corner, he either sees the motionless form of a deer, not a great distance off, regarding him intently before taking flight; or else he hears a sudden crash, and catches a glimpse of the animal as it lopes into the bushes. In either case, he must shoot quickly; but the shot is a close one.

"If he is heard or seen a long way off, the deer is very apt, instead of running away at full speed, to skulk quietly through the bushes. But when suddenly startled, the white-tail makes off at a great rate at a rolling gallop, the long, broad tail, pure white, held up in the air.

"In the dark or in the thick woods, often all that can be seen is the flash of white from the

The old warrior poses with what turned out to be the last big game animal he ever killed—an aggressive bull moose that he took in Quebec in 1915. He shot the enraged bull at 20 feet after it charged him and his guide, Arthur Lirette.

ARCHIBALD RUTLEDGE
THE TROPHY OF A LIFETIME

From "Trophy of a Lifetime," which appeared in the classic book, *Those Were the Days* (1955). One of the greatest whitetail writers of the 20th century, Archibald Rutledge wrote dozens of stories and numerous books about hunting deer on his beloved Hampton Plantation in South Carolina's Low Country. Since colonial days, deer hunting with hounds has been a much-cherished Southern tradition.

It was the day after Christmas in 1942 and Archibald Rutledge was hunting with Prince Alston, his negro foreman and boyhood friend of many years. The two hunters were celebrating the birth of Prince's first son, born on Christmas Day. As they often did, Prince handled the dogs while "Old Flintlock" took a stand. On this memorable day, Rutledge would take home his best buck ever, a huge 13-point "swamp stag."

Prince had brought along two hounds, Red and Queenie. He planned to turn them loose more than a mile away from the spot where Rutledge was waiting.

"For twenty minutes I waited," Rutledge wrote. "Nothing happened. All was silent, serenity, with the quiet woods stretching away boundlessly on all sides. Then, down in the edge of the deep river swamp I heard Prince begin to drive. Almost immediately the hounds started to trail, although I could hear them but faintly.

"Then it happened. Suddenly, silently, spectrally, out of the thick woods before me, there appeared the buck for which I had waited fifty years. (I killed my first when I was nine; and I am now verging on sixty.) He was in front of me, to my left; and as he was coming up a slight incline toward me, I could see nothing but his horns. I knew at once that he had a record head, a twelve- or fourteen-pointer; the height of the tines was spectacular. There were some troublesome bushes between us, but he

"Old Flintlock" poses with one of his favorite deer hounds at his beloved Hampton Plantation in the low country of South Carolina. Photo circa 1942.

kept coming. At fifty yards he stopped, almost concealed; but he did not discover me. On the second I had first seen the tips of his antlers I had raised my gun. On he came, straight for me from the left quarter. At exactly thirty-two yards (a distance that I carefully measured later), he stopped again, facing me. He had literally wedged himself between two big pines, so that nothing but his breast, his neck, and his

An artist's rendering of the "trophy of a lifetime" taken by Archibald Rutledge in 1942, based on his description of the antlers. Rutledge noted, "The spread between beams is twenty-five inches, the circumference of beam at the base, five inches, and the number of points, thirteen. Two of the tines measure eighteen inches and two, seventeen." These are extraordinary measurements indeed for a South Carolina buck. Could it be that the master hunter and writer of deer stories embellished the size of his "lifetime trophy" just a wee bit? He certainly wouldn't be the first deer hunter to do such a thing! Illustration by Cliff Casey.

that these were his death throes that I never left the stump on which I was sitting—never thought of shooting him again. Finally he righted himself, though he was down at the stern, like a vast sinking battleship, but even then I just watched him, sure that he could not go ten yards. Then in a few seconds, it seemed to me, he gained headway, and while I was trying to get up my gun to give him a second barrel, he had vanished into a dense thicket."

Sure he had made a lethal shot, Rutledge found little blood. Wisely he decided to return to his stump and await Prince and the dogs, thus giving the buck plenty of time to expire.

When Prince showed up with Red and Queenie an hour later, they "took the trail with little hesitation." Confident that most of his buckshot pellets had penetrated the buck's neck, but also expressing some doubt since

grand head showed. As I was sitting practically in the open, I thought, *Now or never*.

"With the utmost deliberation I laid the sight of my gun on his lower neck, in front of his heart, and touched the trigger of the left barrel, which is full choke. I was shooting a high-base express shell, chambering twelve buckshot, a load that I have long found to be deadly.

"As was to be expected, at the roar of the gun things happened. That great stag—and he was huge of body—stood almost upright, and then plunged backward. His gigantic struggles beat anything I had ever seen. But I was so certain

Archibald Rutledge and his boyhood friend, Prince, hunt whitetails along a swamp edge in the low country of South Carolina. Photo circa 1940.

Archibald Rutledge spent a lifetime listening to the music of the dogs chasing deer in his native South Carolina swamp "Low Country." Photo circa mid-1940s.

the buck had managed to get away, Rutledge waited nervously with Prince for the dogs to perform their magic.

"Their full-running cry was suddenly hushed; then they began a sharp, yelping bay, as though they had come on the wounded stag. It may appear strange, but few hounds will close with a wounded buck. They will stand off and bay him, but as a rule, they will not go in on him. I have even seen them turn tail and run the minute he turned on them. Indeed, a wounded buck is a fearsome creature to behold, with his hair standing out, his head lowered, and savagery in his aspect.

After a few tense moments, in which the two hunters split up to search for the buck, Prince stumbled upon the fallen giant.

"I had gone perhaps a quarter mile when, from the very center of that wild morass, I heard Prince let loose a jubilant whoop," Rutledge wrote.

"Somehow through that fearful jungle I got to him, after sinking over my boot tops in muck and water. Prone on the edge of an old bank that spans the field lay my 'lifetime' buck. And he was stone dead.

"When we finally got him home, and I had a fair chance to look him over, I knew that he was by far the largest buck I had ever killed, and perhaps the largest I had ever seen.

"I derived a great deal of pleasure in entering his antler measurements in my records: apparently they are a record for South Carolina. The spread between the beams is twenty-five inches, the circumference of beam at the base is five inches, and the number of points, is thirteen. Two of the tines measure eighteen inches and two, seventeen. The antlers are remarkable for their beautiful chestnut color, their heavy beading, and their almost perfect symmetry.

"Perhaps never again shall I have another such experience. But really it paid me to wait for fifty years for a stag like that. And I hope you'll get a chance some day at one just like him."

PAPA FRED BEAR
THE FATHER OF BOW HUNTING

Born in Waynesboro, Pennsylvania in 1902, Fred Bear was to the archery industry what John Browning was to the firearms industry. He was a pioneer, an inventor and an avid bow hunter. Most of all he was a man who was highly respected by his peers because of his integrity, honesty and high standards. Fred was one of America's great ambassadors for hunting and one of the greatest sportsmen to ever live. He stands in a class by himself and definitely deserves to be called the "father of bow hunting."

Fred went on his first whitetail hunt with his dad when he was 13. He shot his first deer with a rifle a year later. During his early 20s, Fred worked several different jobs in the auto industry in Detroit and attended night school.

Fred's interest in archery was inspired when he saw Art Young's bow hunting film, *Adventure in Alaska*, in a Detroit theatre. Fred later met Young and the two men became friends. They started shooting together and making bow hunting equipment in Fred's basement. Art Young's impact in archery was so great that his name was later used when the Pope and Young Club, the nation's keeper of archery big game records, was established.

Fred went bow hunting for whitetails for the first time in 1929. Although Fred aspired to become a great bow hunter just like his hero, Art Young, being left-handed presented a challenge all its own. Fred had to improvise and make much of his own equipment since little left-handed archery equipment was available in the early 1930s.

Out of necessity, he learned how to make his own bows, arrows and strings. It took several years of hard work and practice before he was

Fred Bear shooting the world-famous recurve bow that he spent more than 20 years developing.

good enough to compete in tournaments. When he finally did perfect his shooting skills, there was no stopping him. He won the state archery championship in Michigan in 1934, 1937 and 1939.

Fred shot his first Michigan whitetail with a bow in 1935. He was very instrumental in creating Michigan's first state-wide archery season for whitetails in 1937.

A few years later, in 1942, he became Michigan's first bowhunter to take a whitetail buck on film. Hunting during a heavy snowstorm with Jan Van Coevering of the *Detroit Free Press* who was operating a movie camera, the footage was later used in Fred's first hunting film.

Fred Bear's passion for archery and bow hunting soon became an obsession. In 1933, during one of the worst years of the Great Depression, Fred was temporarily unemployed when the factory he worked in caught fire and shut down for a time. Undaunted, he pooled his resources with a friend, raised $1,200 of working capital, and founded Bear Archery Company in his garage.

The company struggled to get off the ground. World War II followed the Depression, and most Americans had other things on their minds beside recreational archery. Nonetheless, Fred plowed ahead, developing and patenting such noteworthy archery-related items as the Bear razor broadhead, the three-fingered shooting glove, the attachable bow quiver, and fiberglass bow backing that made for a stronger bow. Fred's take-down recurve bow, offered for the first time in 1967, took him 20 years to perfect.

Fred and his wife moved to Grayling, Michigan after the war in 1947. Although it would be years before the company prospered, Bear Archery soon became a nationally recognized manufacturer of archery tackle. This came about in part because of Fred's worldwide exploits. At a time in life when most avid hunters are beginning to wind down their careers, Fred was just getting started. His amazing adventures of the late 1950s and early '60s made him an international bow-hunting legend.

Fred was in his 50s when he began his quest for some of the world's most challenging big game species. You might think he was somewhat of a late bloomer, but he never lacked in energy, determination or grit.

The peak years of his hunting career paralleled a time in history when some of the world's most sought-after species were still legal to hunt. Fred left no stone unturned in pursuing them. His coolness under pressure became legendary.

In 1963, at the age of 61, he shot a Bengal

Papa Bear's amazing life story has been captured in a number of excellent books.

tiger in India. The following year, he arrowed an African elephant at 40 yards. In 1965, he became the second man in history to shoot a male lion with bow and arrow (Art Young had done it several years earlier). Fred also shot a Cape buffalo.

In 1966, he attained a lifelong dream of shooting a polar bear with his recurve bow. The hunt took 25 days. It was his third hunt for a polar bear, one of the world's most dangerous and unpredictable animals. The hunt was featured in an episode of the popular 1960s series *The American Sportsman*.

During his career, Fred established archery world records for a number of species including Canada moose, mountain caribou, barren-ground caribou, Alaskan Kodiak brown bear and stone sheep. Many of his on-camera shots were extraordinary. People still talk about them

Fred poses with a massive Alaskan moose taken in 1966. The huge bull weighed 1,500 pounds.

today. Fred appeared on numerous national TV shows and filmed a number of episodes with *The American Sportsman*.

In1968, Fred sold controlling interest in his company but stayed on as chairman. In 1978, Bear Archery relocated from Grayling, Michigan to Gainesville, Florida. Fred passed away in Gainesville in 1988 at the age of 86. He had suffered from emphysema for a number of years.

Today, some of Fred's famous trophies and artifacts are housed in Johnny Morris' Wonders of Wildlife National Museum & Aquarium in Springfield, Missouri.

Fred Bear was a pioneer in bow hunting for big game and a fearless advocate for hunting and conservation. He once said, "When a deer hunter is in a tree stand with moral values and with the proper hunting ethics and richer for the experience, that hunter is 20 feet closer to God."

The "Father of Bow Hunting" is certainly a well-deserved and a fitting title for a genuine outdoor legend and hero. Like so many of our luminary outdoorsmen who no longer follow the tracks of the whitetail on this good earth, there will never be another Fred Bear.

Fred canoes across a lake with a fine Michigan whitetail. He traveled the world in pursuit of big game, but his real roots were always in his beloved state of Michigan hunting white-tailed deer.

Most hunters would have given up but not Fred Bear. Fred was being filmed by Jack Van Coevering in a blinding snowstorm near Blaney Park, Michigan when he shot this buck. It was the first whitetail hunt by bow ever filmed in Michigan. The date: Friday the 13th, 1942.

LARRY BENOIT
DEER-TRACKER EXTRAORDINAIRE

Artist Steven A. Shannon captured the essence of the Benoit front porch in Duxbury, Vermont during a typical deer season in the 1970s.

Back in the 1960s and '70s, the image of five or six 200-plus-pound bucks with nice racks hanging on Larry Benoit's front porch with hunters wearing green-checked jackets kneeling in the snow in the foreground and holding Remington Model 7600 pump rifles was one of the most recognizable images in all of New England. Larry's front porch stood within spitting distance of a busy highway, and many a gawking motorist almost ran off the road at the sight of so many huge whitetails. Larry Benoit of Duxbury, Vermont was one of the most unusual deer hunters of the mid 20th century. He never sought any kind of fame or public recognition, but it found him through his passion for snow-tracking mature bucks in the late 1960s and throughout the '70s and '80s.

Sports Afield ran several articles about his

legendary exploits in Vermont and across New England, and his name became a household word in deer hunting circles.

In September 1970, *Sports Afield* ran a photo of Larry on the front cover along with the subtitle: "Larry Benoit—Is he the best deer hunter in America?"

This was the first time in the history of the magazine that a live hunter had ever appeared on the front cover of *Sports Afield*. It was a ground-breaking event. At the time, Larry might well have been the best deer hunter in America. If not, he was certainly one of the most unique.

Several more stories were written about Larry in *Sports Afield* in the mid-'70s. In 1975, Larry published his classic book, *How To Bag the Biggest Buck of Your Life*. Today the book is a collector's item and those who own copies treasure them.

During his lifetime, Larry perfected the art of snow-tracking mature whitetail bucks. His great success made him a living legend. Hundreds of hunters tried to mimic his hunting style by wearing the signature green-checkered, wool hunting coat Larry and his sons always wore when they were on the track of a big buck, not to mention using the same type of rifle. Larry romanticized the art of snow-tracking with his traditional Remington Model 7600 .30-06 pump. Remington sold a considerable number of rifles because of his exploits.

But even though mimicry may be the best form of flattery, Larry was in a class by himself. Possessing American Indian blood in his veins and the true pioneer spirit that built this great

The author (left) poses with Larry Benoit, and Larry's trademark rifle, a Remington pump .30-06, in 2006. Larry's home was a living museum filled with many decades worth of racks, trophy mounts, artifacts, old guns, old photos and other priceless deer-hunting treasures.

country, Larry was a throwback to the time of true hunting heroes like Fred Goodwin of Maine and Fred Bear of Michigan.

Larry was a purist in every sense of the word. "It was often said of him that he knew what the deer was going to do before the deer knew it," noted Ron Boucher, a well-known whitetail expert and hunter from Wallingford, Vermont, who called Larry a friend for 30 years. "Larry was to whitetail hunting what Ted Williams was to baseball and Dale Earnhardt was to auto racing. He was a one-of-a-kind. There will never be another one like him."

Craig Jaques is an avid whitetail hunter who also knew Larry for many decades and hunted with him in Quebec. Like so many people who befriended Larry over the years, Craig's initial introduction to the famous hunter was a memorable experience that he would not soon forget.

"I was hunting with my dad when I was 12 years old in 1964," Craig said. "We were coming out of the woods at dark after the day's hunt and we saw this hunter walking down the road. My dad stopped and asked him if he needed a lift. He smiled and said 'Yes.'

"We took him all the way to his house. Once we got there, he invited us inside where we met his wife, Iris. Even back then, the walls were covered with deer antlers. It was the most unbelievable thing I had ever seen. I talked about it to my friends for weeks. He was my hero!"

Although Craig and Larry became very good friends and did many things together, it took another 35 years before Craig actually got to go hunting with the Vermont legend.

"I took him with me to Ontario in 1999, and he fell in love with the place," Craig said. "He saw wolves and eagles, and he found plenty of wilderness to get lost in. It was his kind of place."

Larry's classic book is as relevant today as it was almost 40 years ago. A new printing came out in 2003. Any serious whitetail hunter should get a copy and read it.

Speaking of getting lost, Larry never gave that matter much concern. Once he was on the track of a mature 200-pound buck, he would doggedly stay on the trail until he caught up with his quarry or until darkness forced him to quit for the day. He would be back on the trail at dawn the next morning. Several of his most prized bucks took several days to track down.

Larry did things his way, and it was never easy. A big buck in his eyes had to dress out at more than 200 pounds. Many of his deer dressed in the 250-pound range. Although many of the mature, big-bodied bucks he killed carried outstanding racks, antler size held little interest for him. It was all about tracking and killing mature deer and the challenge of outsmarting a crafty old ridge-runner.

Larry was a natural woodsman and hunter. To demonstrate his determination and single-mindedness, in the old days, when it was bitter cold outside, he would often bring deer right inside the house and skin them out in his living room. Iris never seemed to mind.

Larry continued to hunt right up until the end. He died of cancer in October 2013 at age 89. The very season before, he had killed a good buck in Wisconsin while hunting with one of his sons. Larry inspired countless thousands of hunters through his book and magazine stories. His love of deer hunting and spirit for the great outdoors will always be with every true deer hunter.

During deer seasons back in the 1960s and '70s, this classic scene of five or six big bucks hanging on the Benoit's front porch was one of the most recognizable scenes in Vermont. Photos courtesy of Curtis Smiley, circa 1970.

JACK CROCKFORD'S DART GUN
A WORLDWIDE GAME CHANGER

John Moses Browning (1885-1926) made his first gun out of scrap metal at age 13. Jack Crockford (1923-2011) made his first gun out of wood at age 12. Both men possessed a rare genius for firearms that manifested itself early in their lives. Thanks to his grandfather, Jack's infatuation for guns and hunting was enhanced from an early age. Hailing from Lower Michigan, by the time he was a teenager Jack was an accomplished deer hunter, shooter and a self-taught gunsmith.

Jack spent two years attending Michigan State University before World War II interrupted his college career. He joined the Army Air Corps and became a crack pilot. By war's end, he had flown 423 missions over the "hump" in Burma and China. On more than one occasion, heavy cloud banks over the Himalayas saved his unarmed C-46 cargo plane from the ruthless Japanese Zeroes that were always looking for an easy kill.

Jack was still a kid when he returned home with a handful of medals, a bona fide war hero. He immediately picked up where he had left off at Michigan State. Because of the influence of a special professor, he changed his major and graduated with a degree in wildlife management, one of the first of its kind ever granted in the entire country.

While pursuing his degree in the late 1940s, an idea came to him. What if he could build a special gun designed to shoot a dart containing a tranquilizing agent that could subdue a wild animal? The idea certainly was not new, but it had never been done successfully. If he could do it in this modern age of 20th century wildlife management, the possibilities would be endless. Jack was so obsessed with the idea that he

A gifted craftsman and gunmaker, Jack Crockford holds one of nearly 100 flintlock and percussion rifles he made during his lifetime. He also handcrafted numerous knives and became a skilled engraver. Photo circa 1990.

almost lost his college sweetheart and future wife-to-be over the issue. But the idea would not go away, and fate seemed to step in and help the 24-year-old biologist pursue his dream.

Graduating in late 1947 with a BS degree in wildlife biology, he interviewed for a job with the Georgia Game and Fish Commission as a field biologist. He was hired on the spot by then Game and Fish Commission Director Charlie Elliott, who later became a nationally prominent writer for *Outdoor Life* magazine. (See Chapter 5 for more on Elliott).

Recognizing the potential to reestablish the badly depleted deer herd across Georgia, Jack pushed hard to launch a statewide deer restoration program. That program was initiated in 1950. Live-trapping operations began in the

Jack Crockford poses with one of his early prototype dart guns, a converted Sheridan air rifle, used to tranquilize deer in the mid-1950s. Photo circa 2006.

mountains and on several of Georgia's privately owned coastal islands where deer numbers were high. Flying a state-owned Cessna 180, Jack frequently made runs from one island to another, often landing on the beach at low tide and sleeping in the woods.

In 1952, Jack began working on his idea to develop a dart gun. After months of trial and error, working long hours at night in his basement, he successfully modified a commercial air rifle and developed a primitive dart. After many more months of work, he developed a more sophisticated dart that became widely known as the "flying syringe." Associates at the University of Georgia were instrumental in developing a suitable drug that would tranquilize deer without killing them.

Once perfected, the Crockford "Cap-Chur" gun quickly gained international attention. Wildlife agencies across the world requested rifles that could be used to tranquilize elephants, wild cattle and other large animals.

Being an employee of the state, Jack was not in a position to manufacture his dart gun commercially. A pharmaceutical salesman named Red Palmer saw the potential. He patented the gun with Jack's permission and began selling them around the world, becoming a millionaire in the process. Jack's world-famous Cap-Chur gun is still one of the primary means for taking wild animals alive.

Jack went on to become director of Georgia Game and Fish (now the Department of Natural Resources) under Governor Jimmy Carter in 1971. He retired as director in 1978. A man of many talents, during his lifetime Jack the artist handmade nearly 100 flintlock and percussion rifles. One of his flintlock rifles hung proudly in the oval office during the presidency of Jimmy Carter. Today, Jack's rifles are collector's items fetching many thousands of dollars.

Jack also made hundreds of superb hunting knives, which are also collector's items, and he became a gifted engraver of guns. While his career saw many remarkable achievements, his two greatest accomplishments were the development of the tranquilizer dart gun and the reestablishment of Georgia's white-tailed deer herd. His work with deer earned him the fitting title, "the father of the Georgia deer restoration program."

Jack was a lifelong whitetail hunter who often used primitive rifles. He was also an avid grouse hunter and fly fisherman. He died in 2011 at the age of 88.

An early version of Jack Crockford's "Cap-Chur" gun with "flying syringe" darts, circa late 1950s.

MIKE ALTIZER
A DEER HUNTER'S TALE

Tennessee sportsman and noted outdoor writer Michael Altizer poses with the huge Missouri whitetail that he took in 1954 with his father's hand-me-down Marlin Model 336.

Michael Altizer of Bishop, Tennessee was only 4 years old when his dad, Claude, brought home the first deer young Michael had ever seen. Claude had taken the eight-point buck in Carroll County, Virginia in the autumn of 1954 with a Marlin Model 336. Claude purchased the rifle in .35 Remington the day he returned from the Korean War.

When his dad told him he was going on a deer hunt, young Michael expected him to bring home something the size of a rabbit or a groundhog, animals he was used to seeing, but not a creature three times larger than he was. Michael was in awe of his dad's first trophy for a long time.

Fast forward 50 years. After considerable use, the old Marlin was passed down from father to son. With the rifle still in excellent condition, Michael picked up where his dad left off. Over time, he bagged deer, bear and boar while hunting with the cherished old gun. Later on, he incorporated many of those hunts into his widely read magazine and much-heralded stories and books written for *Sporting Classics*.

A few years back, Michael took this outstanding buck in Missouri using his dad's heirloom rifle. "I was carrying the original snapshot of him and me with his first buck in my coat pocket at the time I shot the deer."

Needless to say, that Missouri hunt was

special in more ways than one. When the time comes, Michael plans to entrust the old Marlin to his nephew, Gabe, thus adding another chapter to a timeless family story. Now 8 years old, Gabe has become one of Michael's favorite outdoor companions and has grown into quite an impressive deer hunter and fly fisherman in his own right.

This special story illustrates one of the many reasons American hunters have flocked to the autumn woods for well over a century. It is why so many Americans both past and present are truly blessed to call themselves deer hunters.

Michael Altizer, only 4 at the time, was overwhelmed to see the first deer his father, Claude, had ever killed.
Below: Michael shows the old Marlin rifle to his nephew, Gabe, who might be the next owner of the prized rifle.

"The old man paused to light his pipe, and then he turned around and pointed the stem at me.

"'You, boy,' he said. 'By this time you know a lot about guns, but you don't know a lot about guns and deer together. Many a man loses his wits when he sees a big ol' buck bust out of the bushes with a rockin' chair on his head. Trained hunters shoot each other. They get overexcited and just bang away into the bushes. Mind what I say. A deer ain't a deer unless it's got horns on its head and you can see all of it at once. We don't shoot does and we don't shoot spike bucks and we don't shoot each other. There ain't no sense to shootin' a doe or a young'un. One buck can service hundreds of does, and one doe will breed you a mess of deer. If you shoot a young'un, you haven't got much meat, and no horns at all, and you've kept him from breedin' to make more deer for you to shoot. If you shoot a man, they'll likely hang you, and if the man is me, I will be awful gol-damned annoyed and come back to ha'nt you. You mind that gun, and don't pull a trigger until you can see what it is and where it is. Mind, I say.'"

Robert Ruark
The Old Man and the Boy (1957)

NATURE'S MOST ENDURING ART

The great antler collector Widmer Smith of Wisconsin once wrote, "Art lovers take notice . . . kings, queens, prizefighters, popes and gladiators, Indian chiefs and Miss America's—all have to take a back seat to the crown worn by a great whitetail buck."

In reference to antler scores, he went on to write, "Who's to judge nature's art. Perhaps the same panel that judges the Miss America Pageant, or you and I . . . as beauty is in the eye of the beholder."

This incredible specimen of "nature's art" was taken by avid whitetail hunter and long-time Minnesota farmer James Matter on his farm near Callaway in November 1973. With 17 very symmetrical points on each side, the Becker County giant scored 258 2/8 non-typical points. The buck's rack became a new state record and ranked sixth in the world. This deer is definitely a prime sample of nature's art.

Note: Born in 1911 in North Dakota, J. Widmer Smith was one of a handful of nationally renowned antler collectors in the 1940s, '50s and '60s. He was also a lifelong hunter. As one of the premier "horn men" of the 20th century, his knowledge about whitetails was extraordinary. He owned a number of outstanding whitetail racks from Minnesota and the Upper Midwest.

CHAPTER 16

REFLECTIONS: SUNSETS AND NEW HORIZONS

ENDLESS BOUNTY
Numerous turkeys hang on the meat pole along with several deer and a single coyote, indicating this woods-wise group of veteran hunters is probably hunting for profit. The spoils will likely go to nearby city markets. Photo circa 1885.

The whitetail's impact on America's early history and growth is staggering. Long before the first Europeans came ashore in the New World, deer were hunted for food by virtually all of the Eastern Indians. Local tribes used every part of the whitetail's body for some important purpose—meat, bones, skin and antlers. Nothing went to waste. The early settlers who came to America quickly followed their red brother's example. Venison became an essential food item for many of the hungry pioneers and settlers.

Deer hides became one of the new World's most valuable commodities. By the mid-1700s, explorers and "long hunters" like Daniel Boone were penetrating the western frontier in search

HOW MUCH HAS REALLY CHANGED?
This imposing image might easily have been taken a century ago. In truth, this meat pole full of impressive racks is a 1980s photo captured at Michigan's famed Sanctuary Ranch. How much has really changed in the past 100 years?

of pelts and skins for the ever-expanding market. Traders were soon traveling to the back country and bartering for skins with various Indian tribes up and down the Eastern Seaboard. From the mid-1600s to the early 1800s, millions of deer hides were shipped to England from the colonies. By 1850, market hunting had drastically reduced deer numbers over much of the eastern U.S. By 1900, deer populations in most eastern states were at an all-time low.

Protection through game laws and buck limits saw whitetails rebound in many areas during the early 1900s. Despite low numbers in some areas, the golden days of deer hunting in America covered the last few decades of the 1800s and the first few decades of the 20th century. By then, deer were no longer hunted out of necessity by pioneers for food. Although hunters were still motivated to bring home a supply of the delicious meat deer provided, sport hunting for whitetails came into its own.

Deer were found just about everywhere east of the Rocky Mountains, and people from all walks of life could enjoy pursuing an animal that was challenging and exciting to hunt.

Thousands of Americans began to invade the fall deer woods each year. For the first half of the 20th century, the so-called "sport" of deer hunting grew at a steady pace. With new technology, new research material and an increasing knowledge about how to hunt America's No. 1 big game animal, a new surge in whitetail hunting began in the late 1970s and early '80s, the likes of which had never before been seen in the U.S.

Some prominent outdoor writers termed this unprecedented deer craze a "cult." Among other things, this new craze included a passionate enthusiasm for trophy hunting, antler collecting, deer farming, shed antler collecting and making replica antlers of notable deer. A number of respected writers predicted the momentum could not last more than a few years.

Not only did it last, the whitetail frenzy continued through the 1990s and into the early 2000s with no slowdown in sight.

By coincidence, whitetail populations in most states had begun to peak at their highest numbers in history due in part to good management by state agencies. Whitetail hunting suddenly became a multi-billion dollar industry. Countless new products began to flood the market—camouflage clothing, tree stands, trail cameras, new innovations in firearms and archery equipment; gadgets of every description. Dozens of new how-to books were published and numerous magazines catering to whitetail hunters flooded the newsstands.

The late 1980s saw the beginning of the video age as hundreds of deer-hunting videos were produced. The early 1990s saw the advent of numerous cable TV shows exclusively catering to whitetail hunting.

Trophy hunting became big business. Outfitters and guiding services sprang up across the country in record numbers, especially in "big deer" states. Annual deer shows drawing huge crowds were established in many cities. Deer management associations were formed, and the research being conducted at prominent universities on whitetails reached new levels.

Despite the naysayers who predicted some sort of "crash" in the early 2000s, whitetail hunting continued to prosper. The recession of 2009 certainly slowed down the momentum in all areas, but it came back stronger than ever.

How much has really changed in the last 130 years? Good or bad, interest in deer hunting has reached heights never before thought possible. In fact, the world as we knew it a generation or so ago has changed in ways we never before thought possible. Where it was once a natural progression for a young boy or girl to start hunting with dad or granddad as soon as he or she was old enough to handle a gun, we now have to make a concentrated effort to get young people away from computer games and out the door. To complicate matters, older hunters are hanging up their guns in record numbers, and younger men and women are not being exposed to the privilege of hunting, fishing and spending time outdoors as they were a few decades ago.

The future of deer hunting has much promise but significant challenges lay ahead. Whitetails are still the greatest hunting challenge on earth! For the past 400 years, the destiny of this country and almost every American citizen has had some sort of connection with white-tailed deer. This is still the case in many areas. Let's hope it always stays that way. In the meantime, Watch your topknot and keep your powder dry!

"A hunting camp is one of the few places left to us where we can dream of a near-perfect tomorrow. Where the harsh realities of lost riches and faded glories can be forgotten and the dreams of what might come down to a delightful day with not too much wind, a crisp morning silvered with frost, and find us—at long last—with the right gun, shells, dogs, and friends who will be pleased forever to remember the day we 'did it all.'

Our greatest trophies are not things, but times.

If in a single day we smell coffee, dawn, gun oil, powder, a wet dog, woodsmoke, bourbon, and the promise of a west wind for a fair tomorrow—and it's possible for us to reek 'happy'—that's just what we will do."

Gene Hill (1928-1997)

LEAN AND MEAN

These men seem serious about collecting their venison, and apparently they know what they are doing. Pictured are at least two lever-action carbines (one an early Winchester Model 94) and three Savage Model 99s. The second man from left is holding several squirrels and two frying pans. You can almost smell the rich squirrel stew simmering over the open fire. This hardy bunch will eat well tonight and have plenty of tales to tell. Photo circa 1910.

THE MOST BREATHTAKING SIGHT IN ALL OF NATURE!

REFLECTIONS: SUNSETS AND NEW HORIZONS

Featuring America's Best Outdoor Writers . . .

The Greatest Deer Hunting Book Ever
Edited By Jim Casada

There's something about the deer-hunting experience, indefinable yet undeniable, which lends itself to the telling of exciting tales. *The Greatest Deer Hunting Book Ever* offers abundant examples of the manner in which the quest for whitetails extends beyond the field to the comfort of the fireside. It features 43 sagas ranging from exciting true-life hunts to wonderfully compelling works of fiction.

The book's 465 pages showcase a stellar lineup of some of the greatest names in American sporting letters, including William Faulkner, Robert Ruark, Archibald Rutledge, Gene Hill, Jack O'Connor, Gordon MacQuarrie and many others.

As you read their works, you'll chuckle, feel a catch in your throat or a tear in your eye, and venture vicariously afield with hunters who know how to take readers to the setting of their story. On these pages, the deer season is always open and the sport's joys endlessly unfold.

The Greatest Deer Hunting Book Ever is available in a hardcover Collector's Edition and a Deluxe Edition limited to 350 numbered copies bound in leather and with gilded endsheets. Editor Jim Casada has signed both editions.

Collector's Edition: Hardcover book with dust jacket. **$40**
Deluxe Edition: 350 leather-bound books, signed & numbered by Jim Casada. **$70**

SportingClassicsStore.com
Order Online or by Phone: **(800) 849-1004**